Tavistock and Innerkip Ontario and Area in Colour Photos, Saving Our History One Photo at a Time

Photography
by Barbara Raué
©2019

Series Name: Cruising Ontario

Book 237: Tavistock and Innerkip and East Zorra-Tavistock Township

Cover photo: 52 Woodstock Street South, Tavistock, Page 5

©All the photos in this book have been taken with my cameras. I own the rights to them.

Series Name: Cruising Ontario
Saving Our History One Photo at a Time
in colour photos

Book 5: Chesley – black and white
Book 10: Dundalk – black and white

Book 44: Drumbo and Area
Book 45: Sheffield and Area
Book 48: London
Book 53-55: Dundas
Book 60: Waterdown
Book 62: Stoney Creek
Book 66: Ancaster and Mount Hope
Book 87-91: Hamilton
Book 92-93: Owen Sound
Book 94: Oakville
Book 96: Mount Forest
Book 113: Waterford and Area
Book 182-183: Burford and Area
Book 237: Tavistock, Innerkip and East-Zorra – Tavistock Township – in colour photos

East Zorra-Tavistock is a township in southwestern Ontario formed on January1, 1975 through the amalgamation of the Township of East Zorra and the Village of Tavistock. It is part of Oxford County.

Tavistock is located 15 kilometres southeast of Stratford and five kilometres south of Shakespeare on County Road 59. In 1848, Captain Henry Eckstein founded Tavistock. The world championship crokinole tournament has been held here annually since 1999.

Innerkip is located on Oxford Road 29 north of Highway 401, northeast of Woodstock.

Huntingford is located on County Road 59, north of Woodstock, west of Innerkip.

Punkeydoodles Corners is located four miles east of Tavistock. Today the corner has a scattering of houses and farms. At one time it was a bustling stop along the Huron Road. The most popular legend about how it got its name is from the song "Yankee Doodle Dandy" which was popular in the 1800s and often sung around the piano at the inn and tavern located at the Corner during the late nineteenth century. Today, the corner is the meeting place of three districts – Oxford County, Perth County and the Region of Waterloo.

Hickson is located at the intersection of Highway 59 and County Road 8, about thirteen kilometers north of Woodstock and ten kilometers south of Tavistock. Hickson was founded in 1876 when the Port Dover and Lake Huron Railway created a whistle-stop here. The new village was named after Sir Joseph Hickson, the general manager of the Grand Trunk Railway.

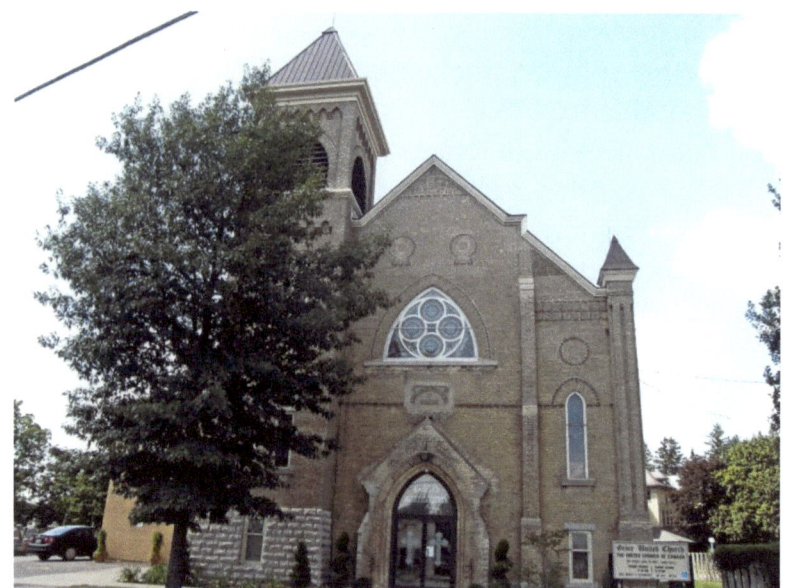

42 William Street (corner of Woodstock Street) - beautiful rose window, fancy brickwork for decoration, buttresses

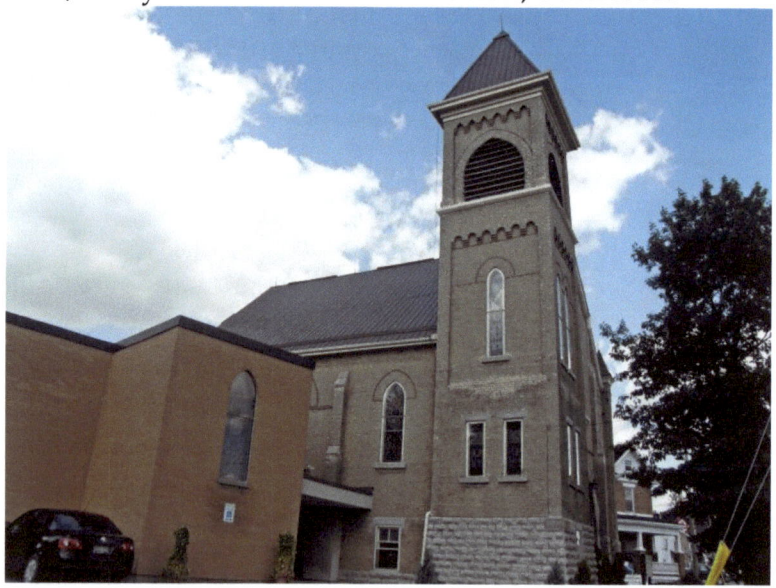

(Original name Zion Evangelical Church) - Grace United Church, Tavistock – built 1904

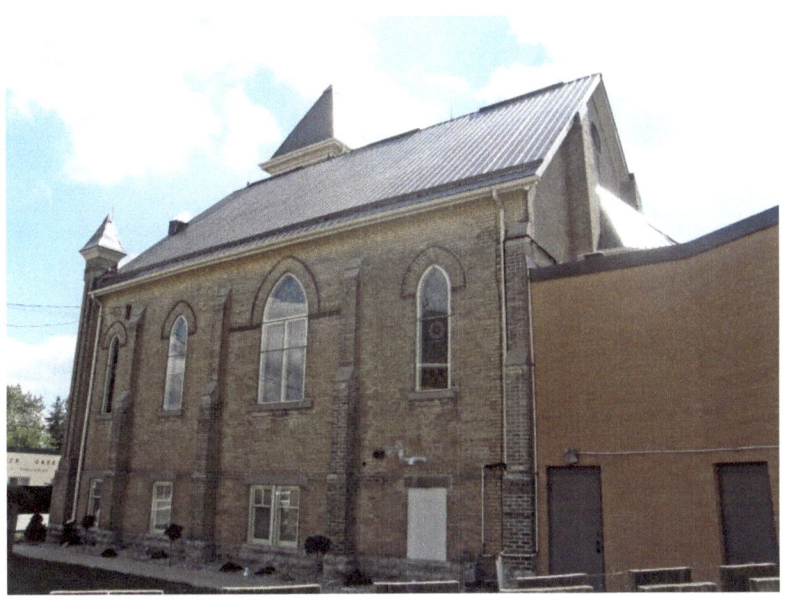

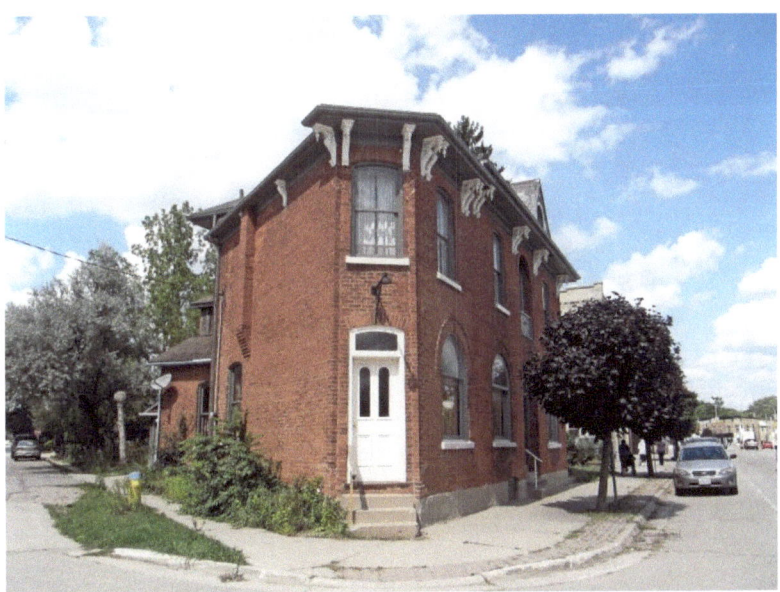

52 Woodstock Street South - The Glass Swan – This late Italianate style has existed since 1892 when Dr. Otto Niemeier bricked over two adjoining structures. This residence is one of the oldest remaining in Tavistock and was the location of several early merchants and doctors.

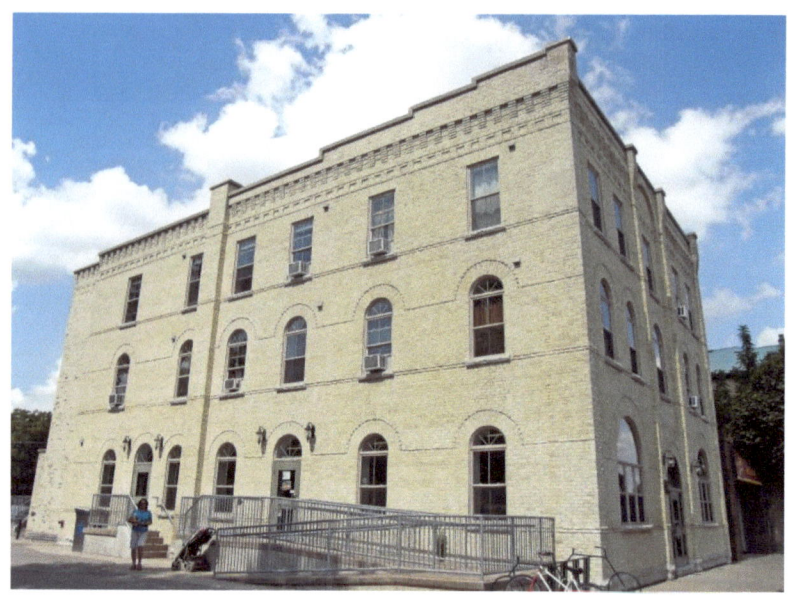

Woodstock Street South – stepped parapet, dentil molding, pilasters, banding, voussoirs

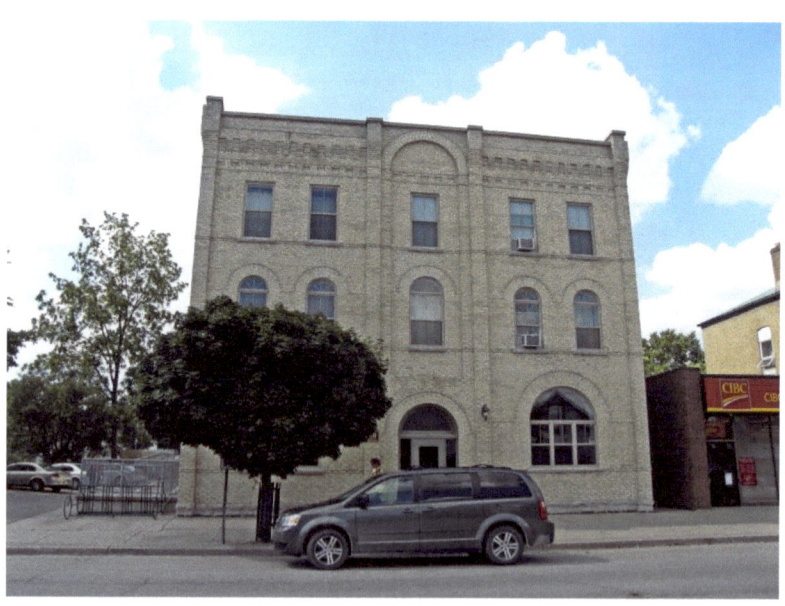

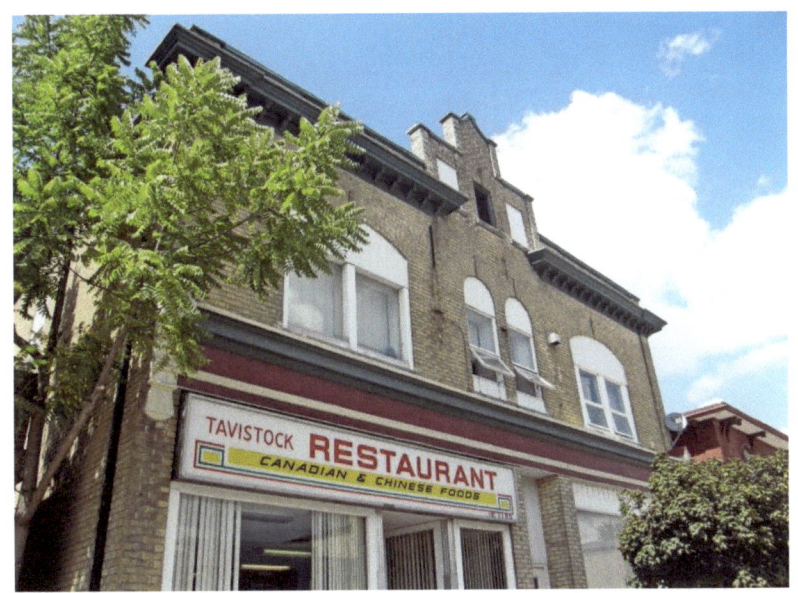

36 Woodstock Street South

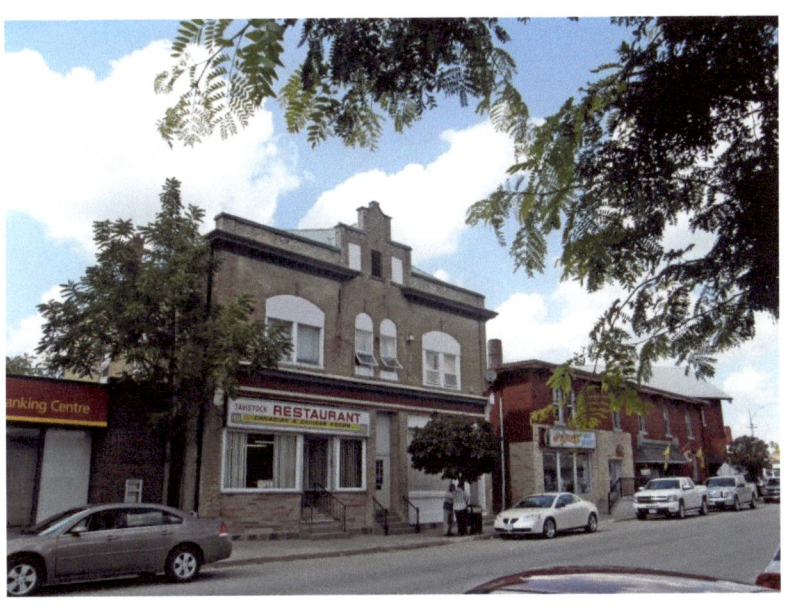

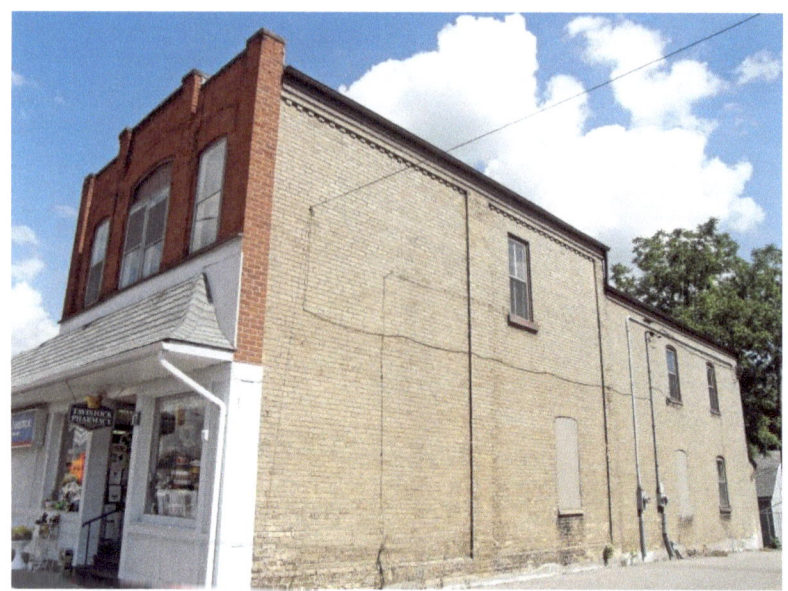

17 Woodstock Street South – Tavistock Pharmacy

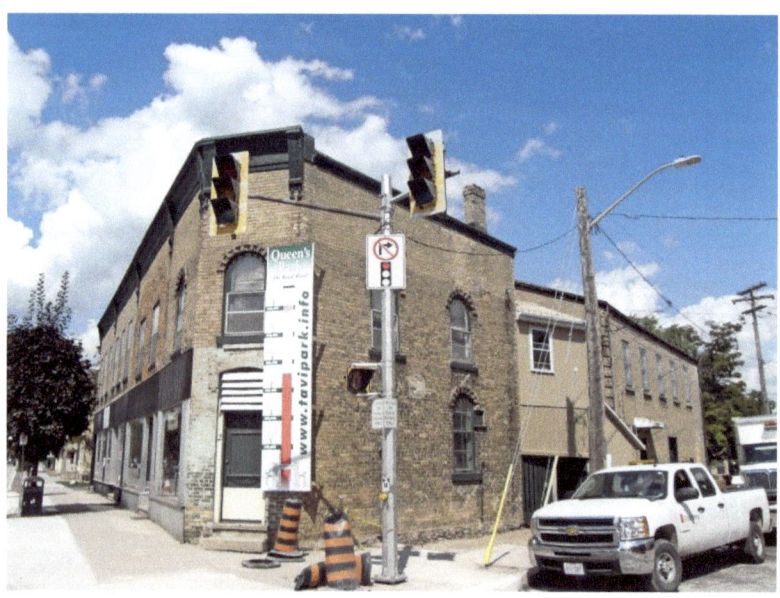

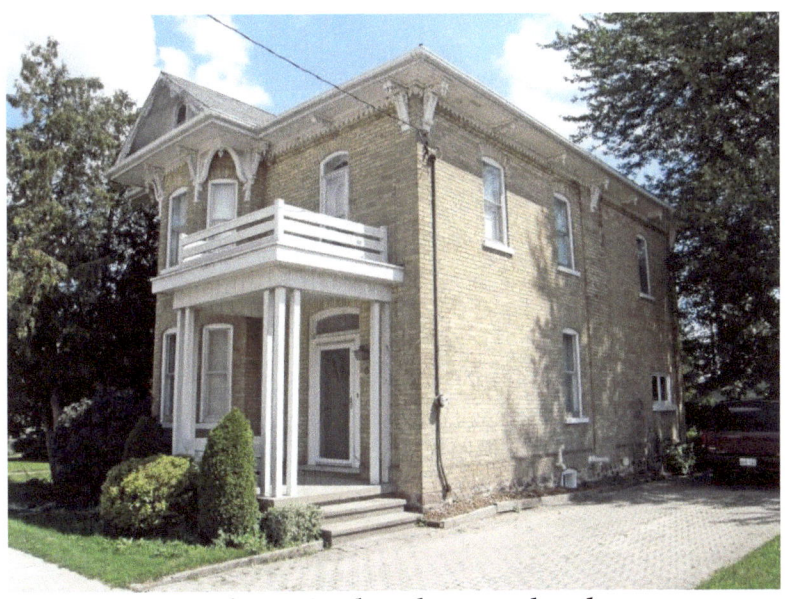
#6 - paired cornice brackets under the eaves

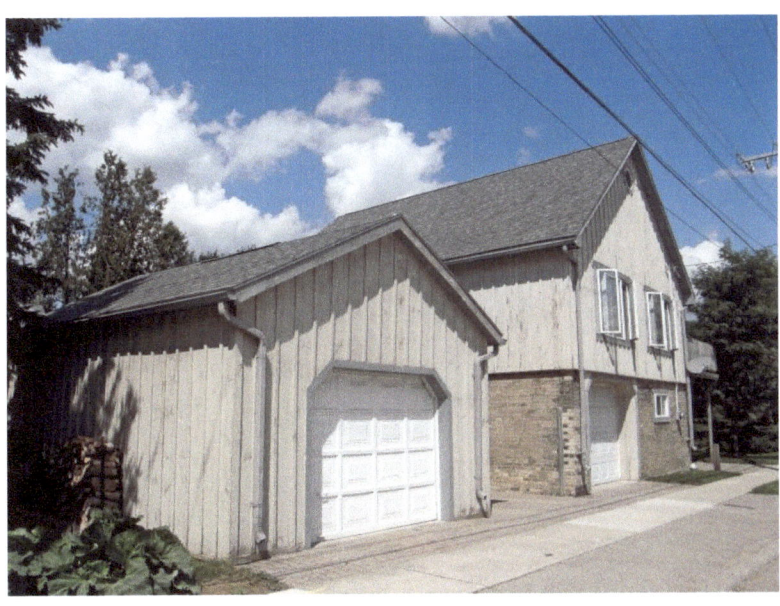

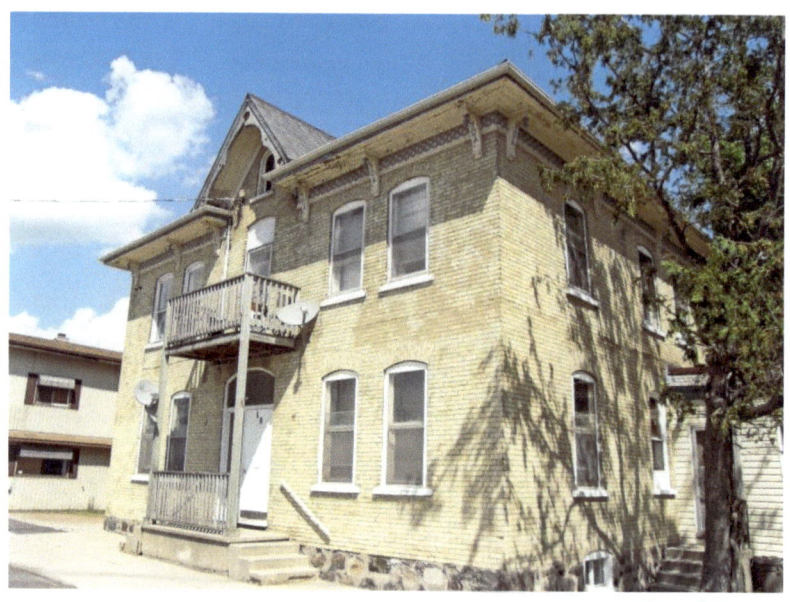

#18 - gingerbread (verge board) around gable, single cornice brackets, decorative cornice

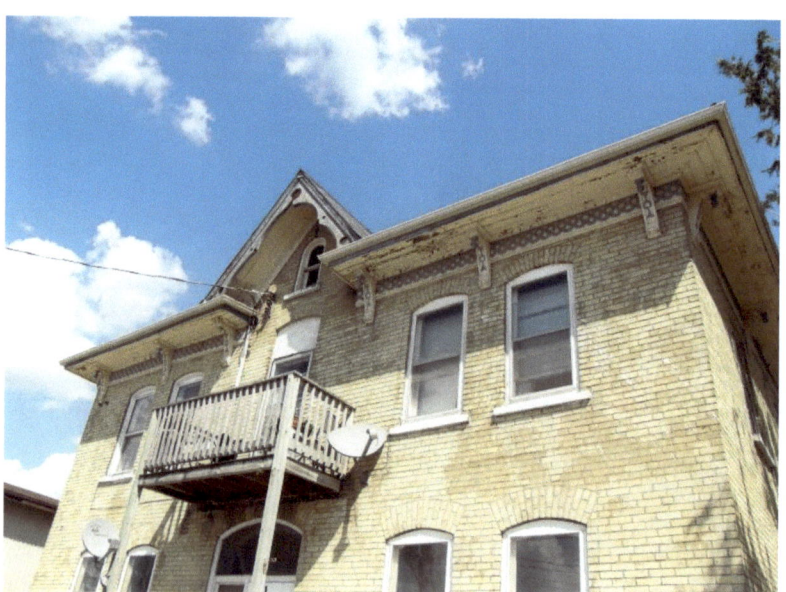

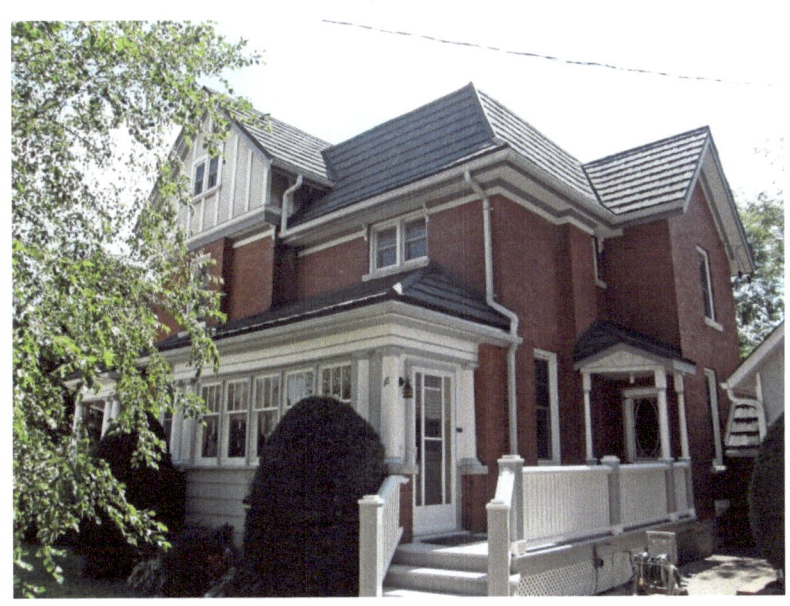

#18 – Queen Anne style – three-story tower, Doric pillars supporting veranda with pediment

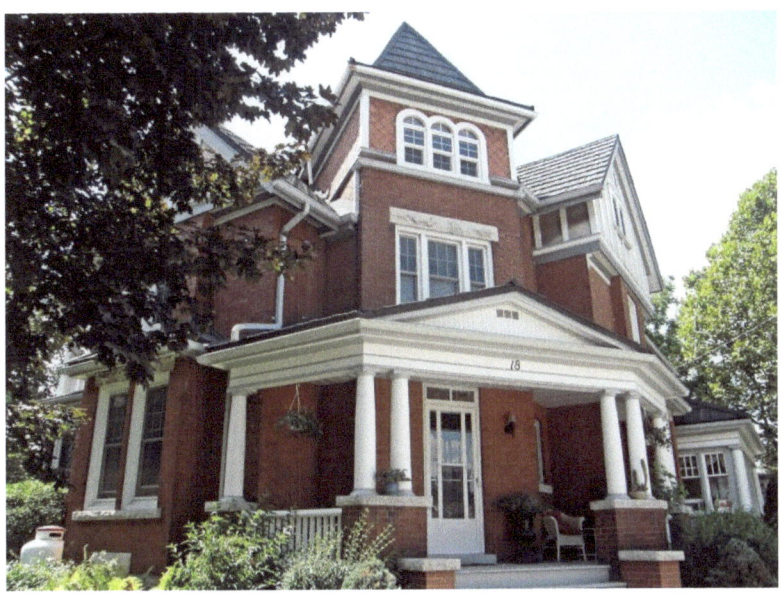

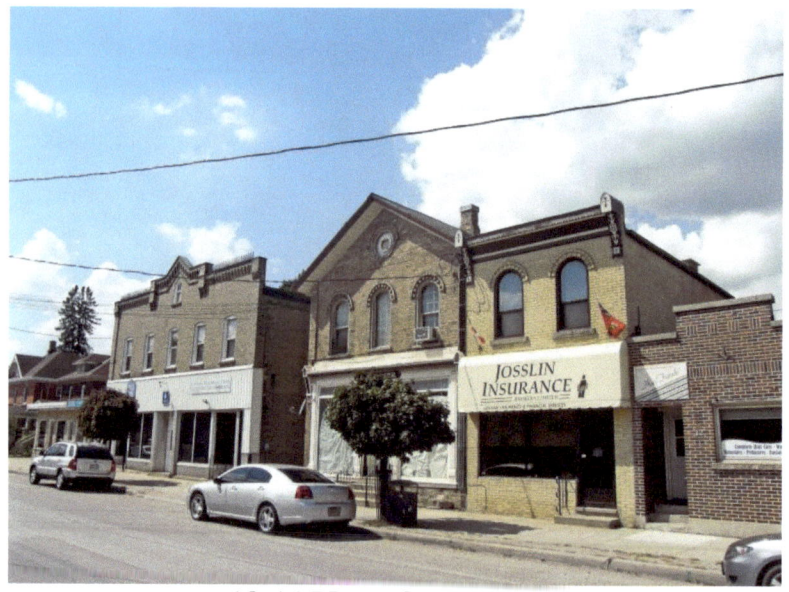
18-14 Hope Street West

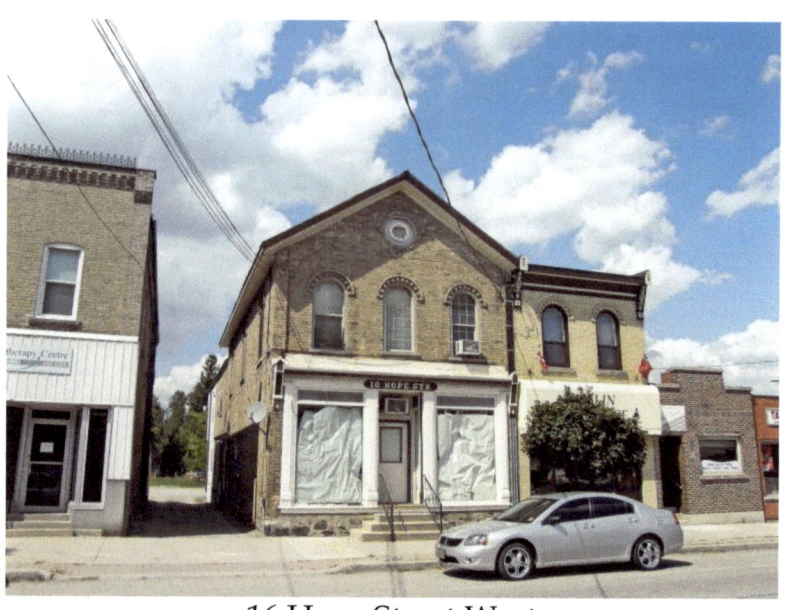
16 Hope Street West

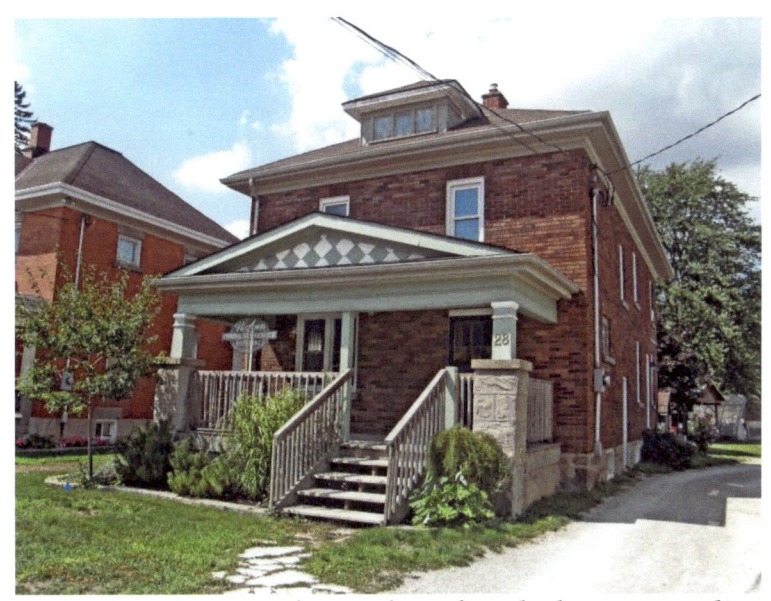

28 Hope Street West – hipped roof with dormer, pediment

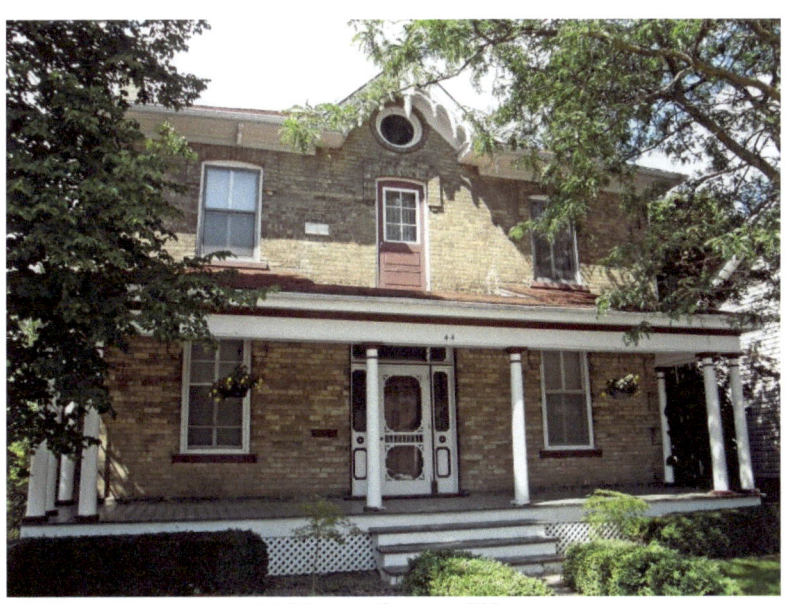

44 Hope Street West

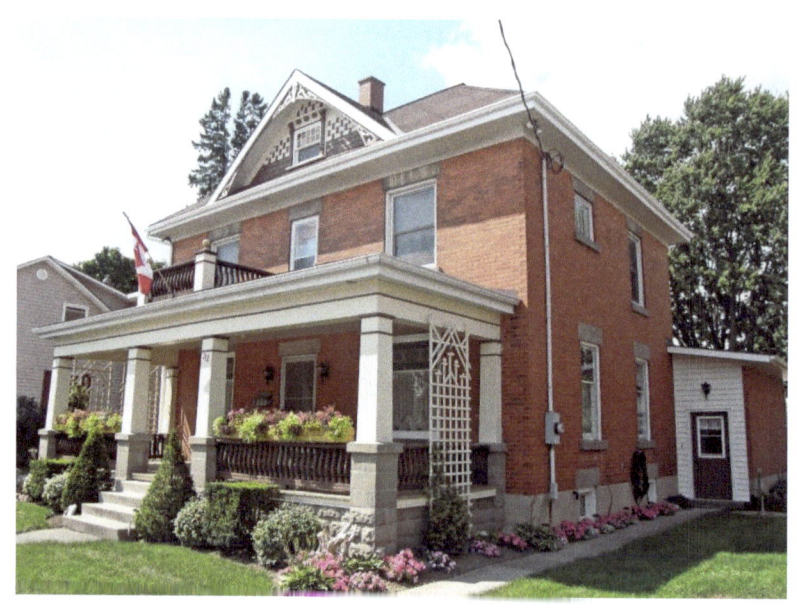

32 Hope Street West

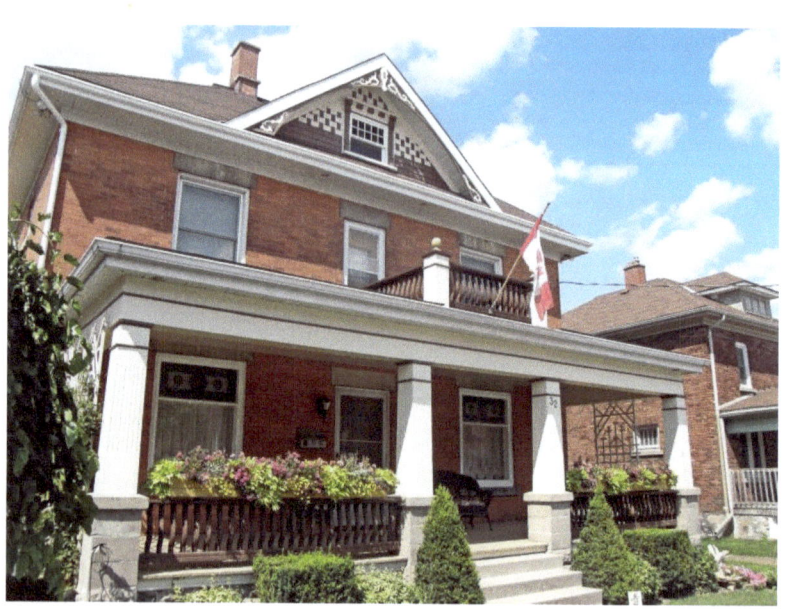

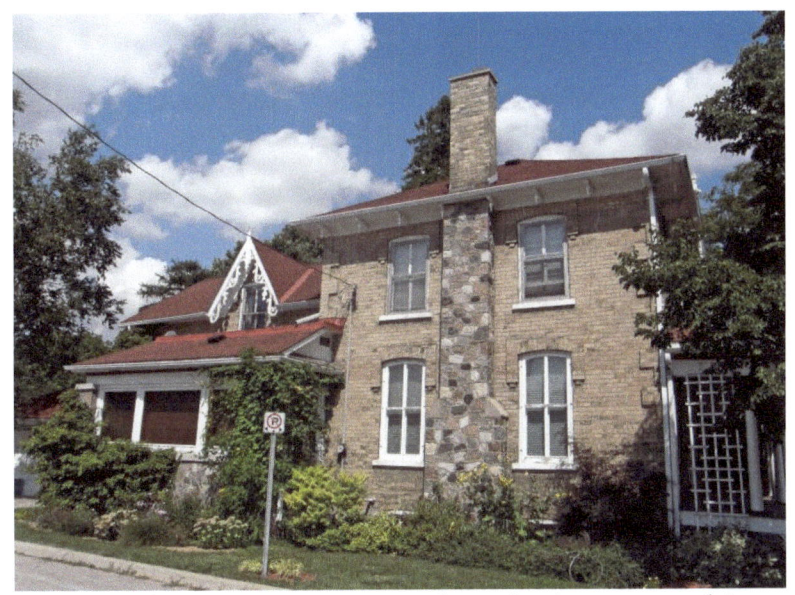
Yellow brick, two storey, verge board trim, stone chimney

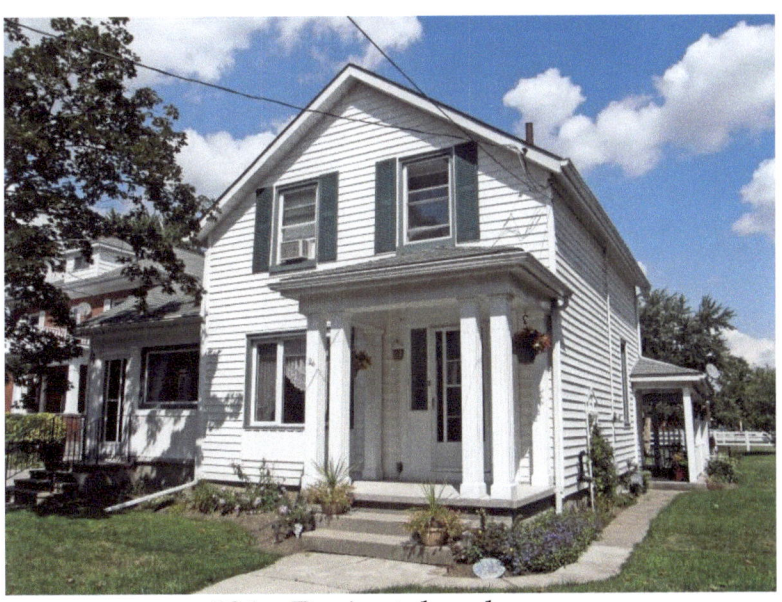
#24 – Doric style columns

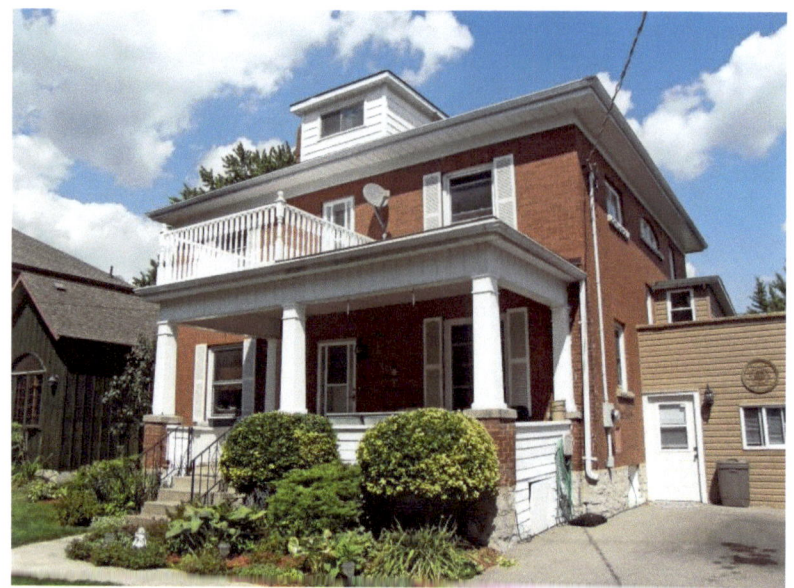
#30 dormer in hipped roof, second-floor balcony

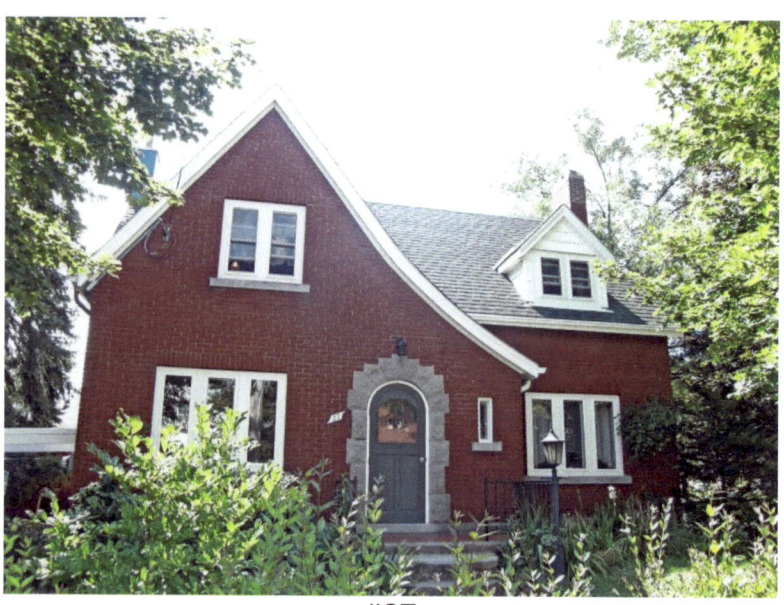
#27

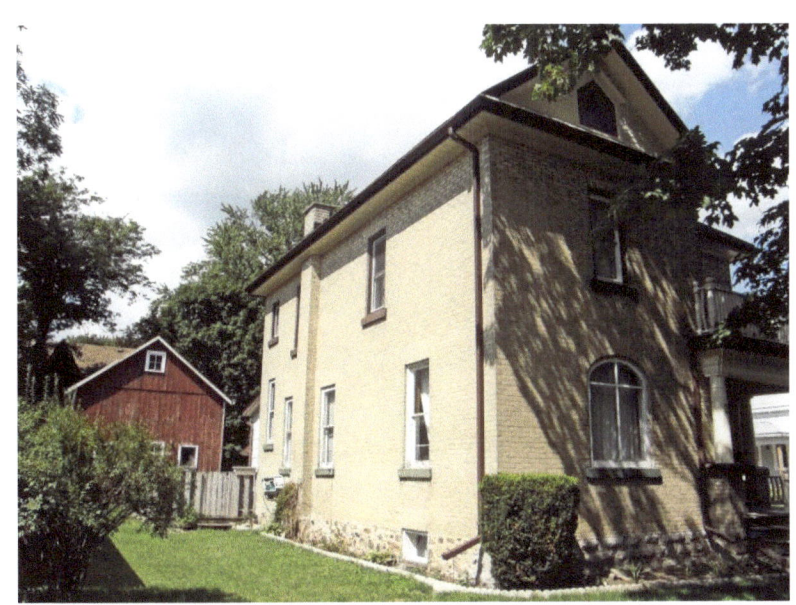

Stone basement

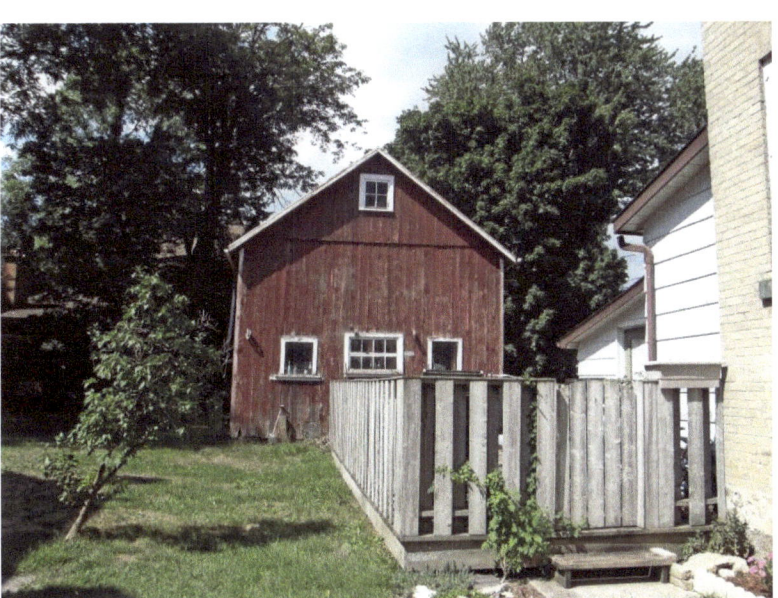

Old wooden shed

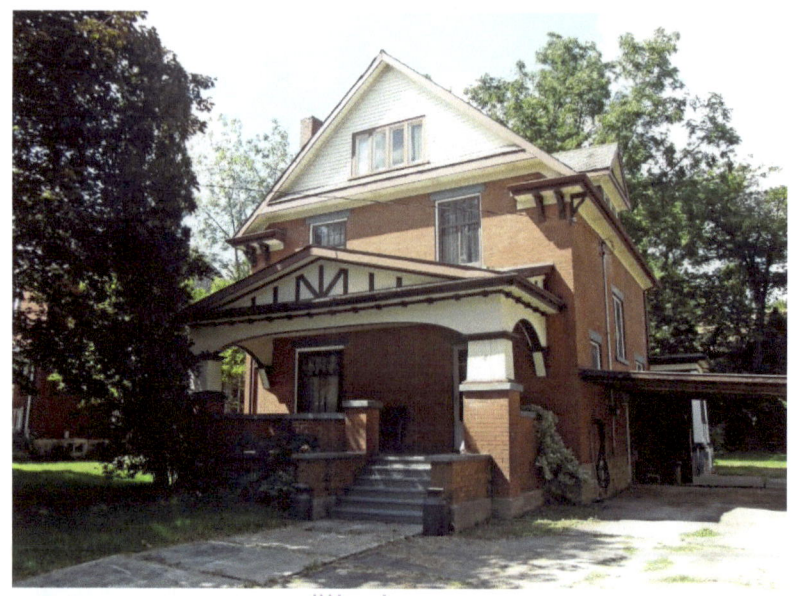

#8 - dormers

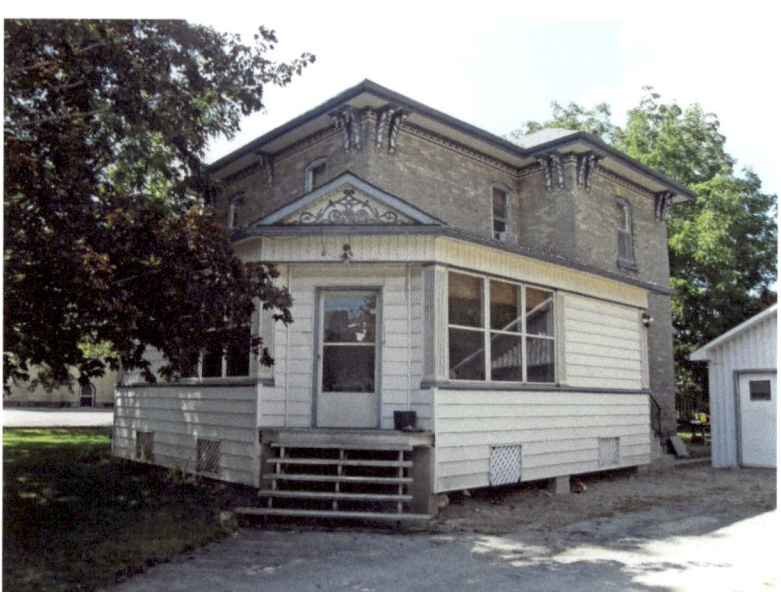

Paired cornice brackets and fancy work in the pediment above door

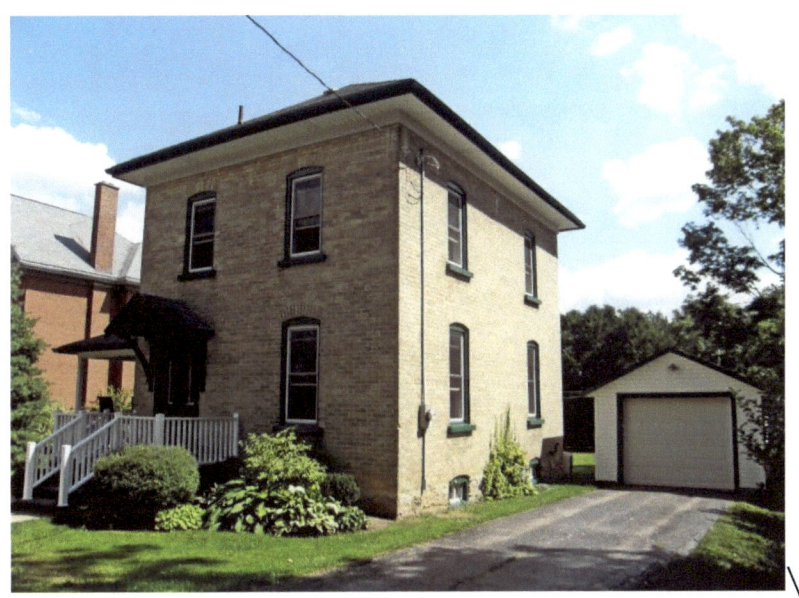
Yellow brick, two storey, hipped roof

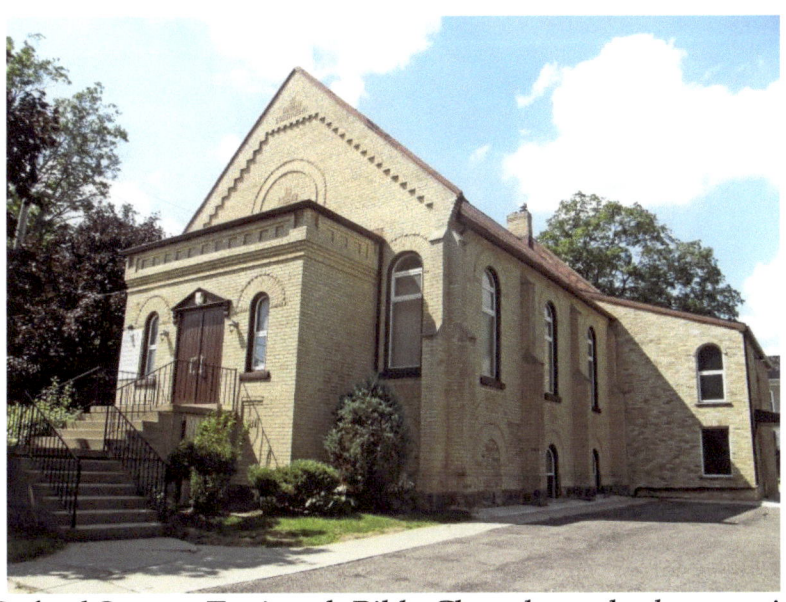
32 Oxford Street - Tavistock Bible Chapel – arched voussoirs over windows

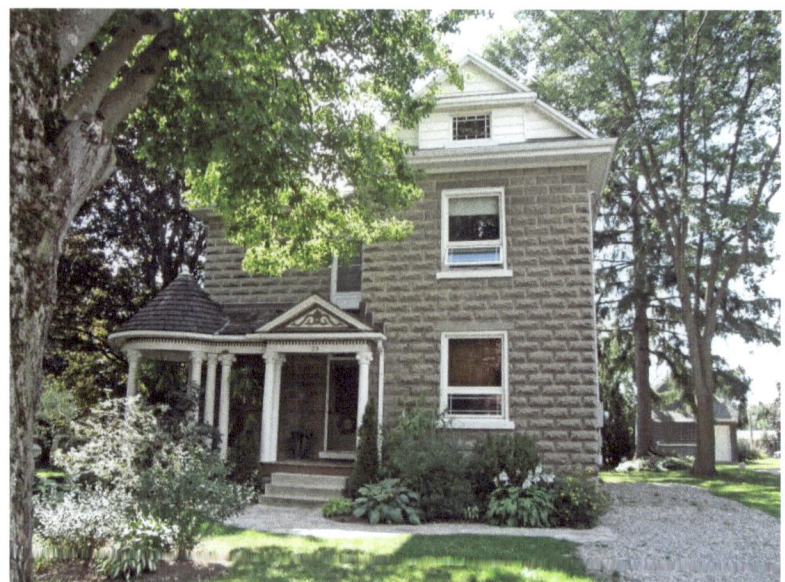

#39 – decorative tympanum, Neoclassical pillars supporting veranda

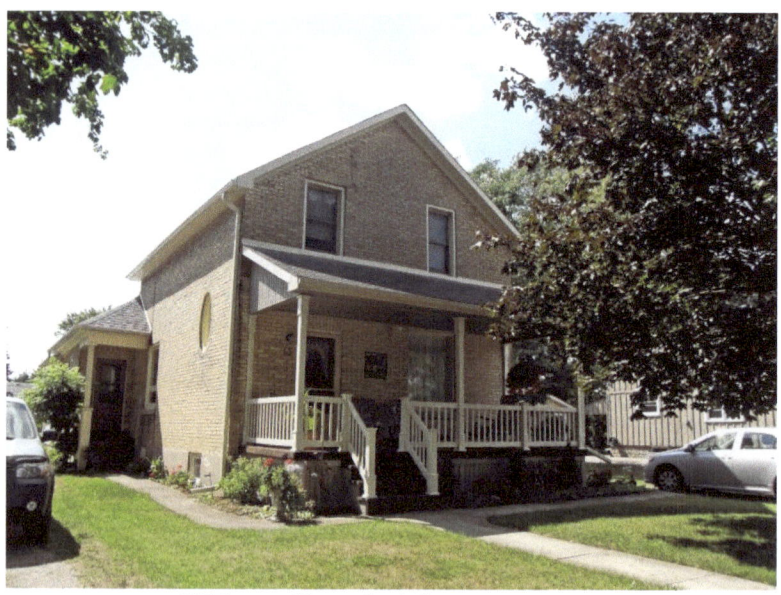

#55 – yellow brick, two storey

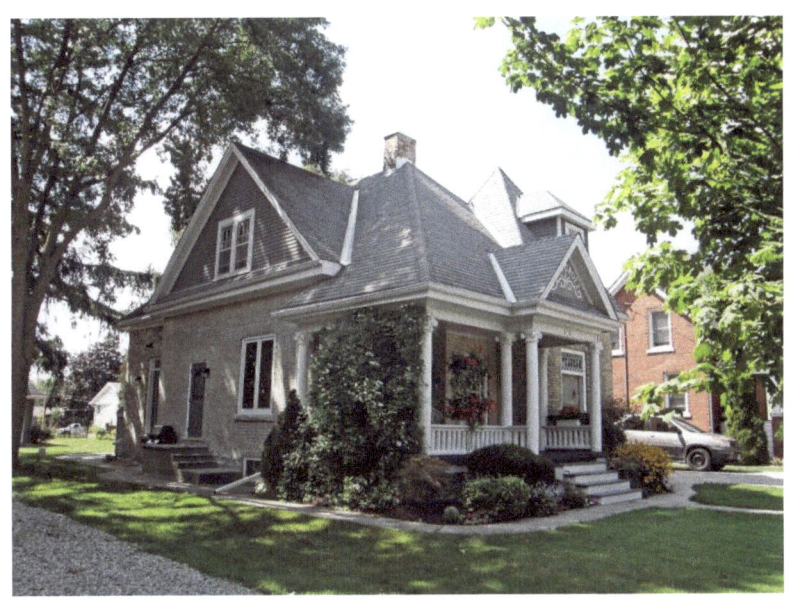

45 – Hillcroft - A lovely yellow brick Queen Anne, with an interesting variation of roof pitches; beautiful Neoclassical pillar details

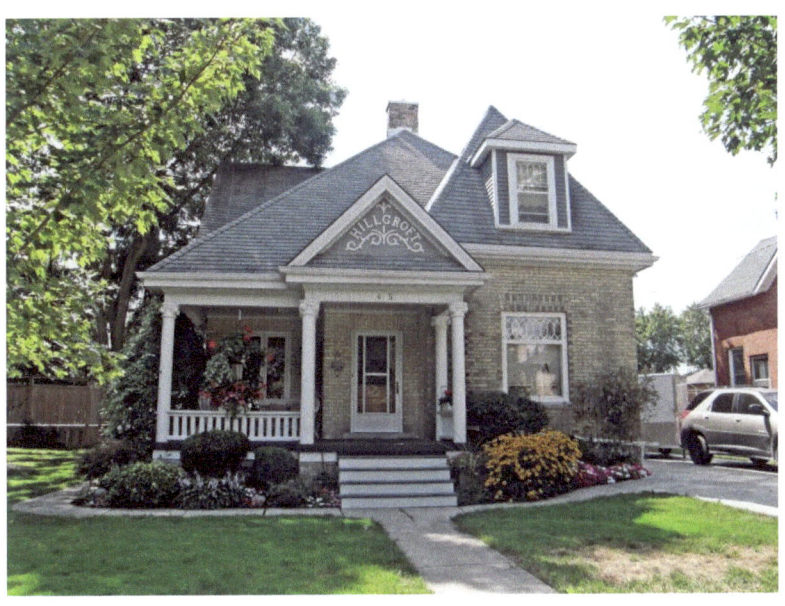

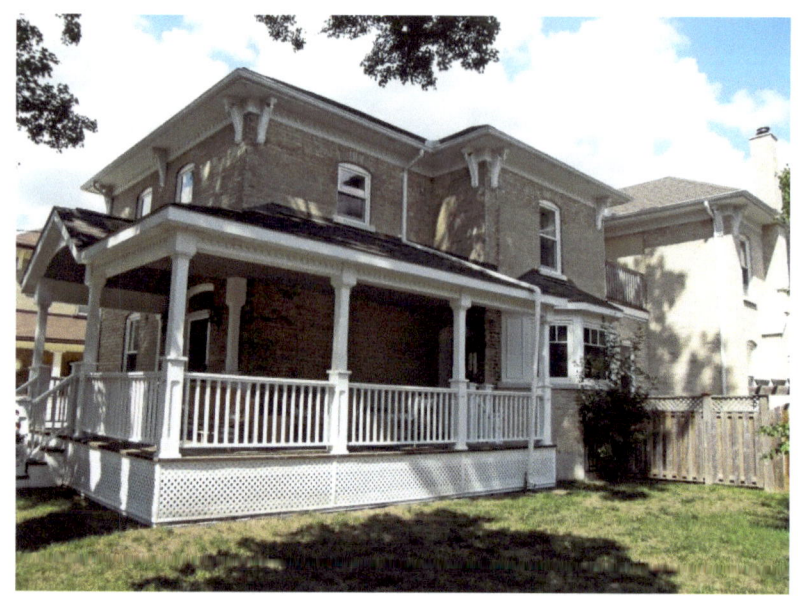

#54 – cornice brackets, wraparound veranda

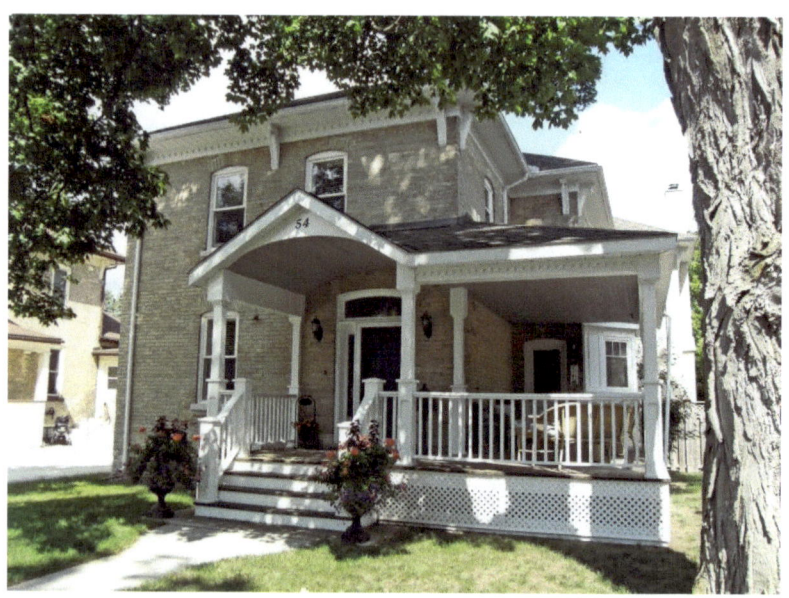

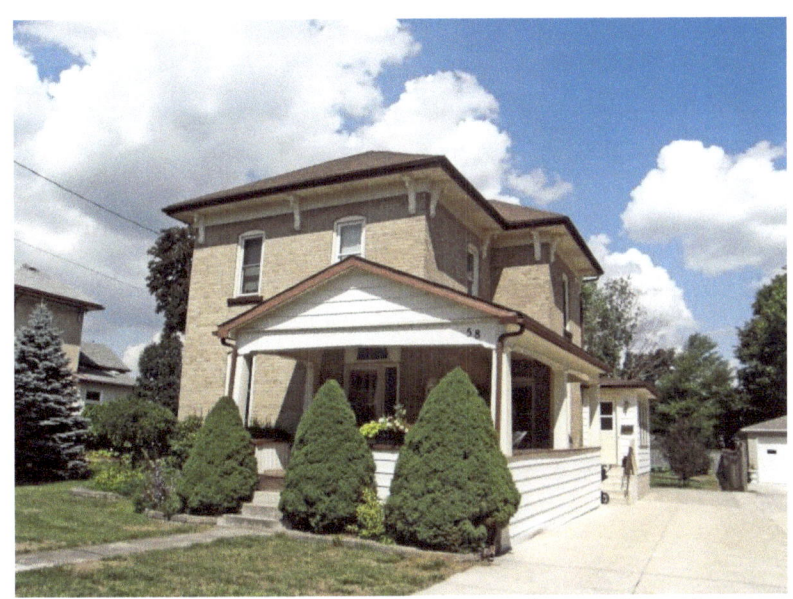
#58 – single cornice brackets, hipped roof

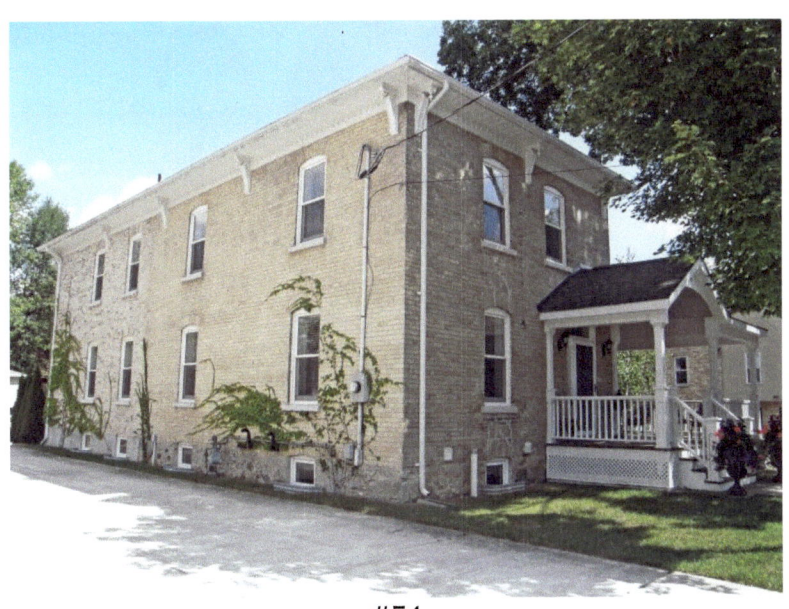
#54

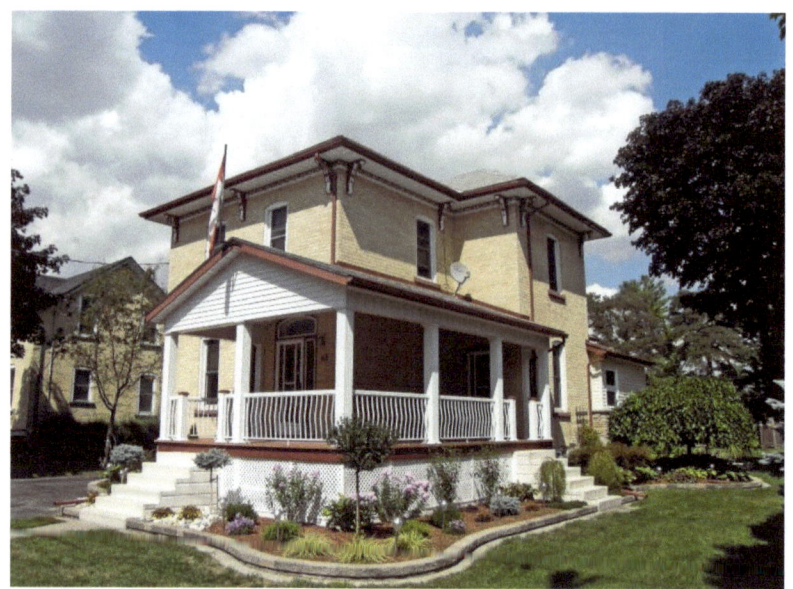

#68 – yellow brick

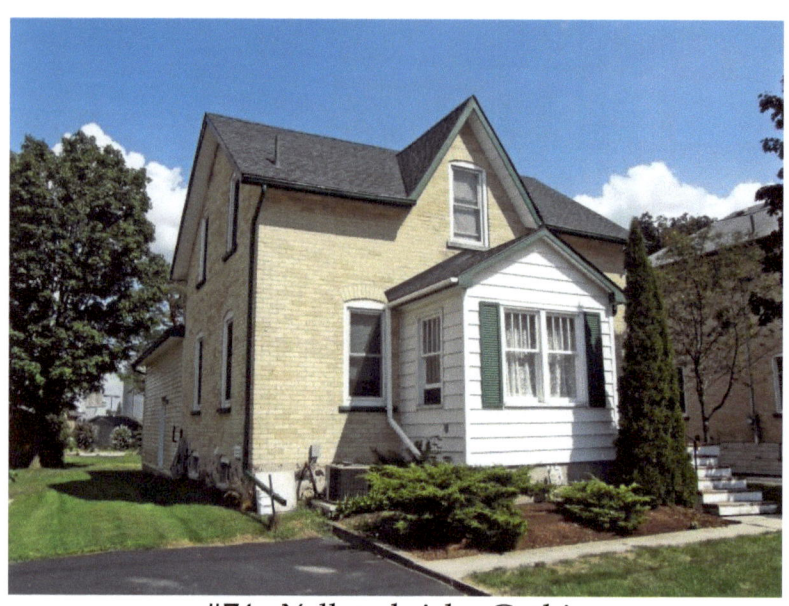

#74 - Yellow brick - Gothic

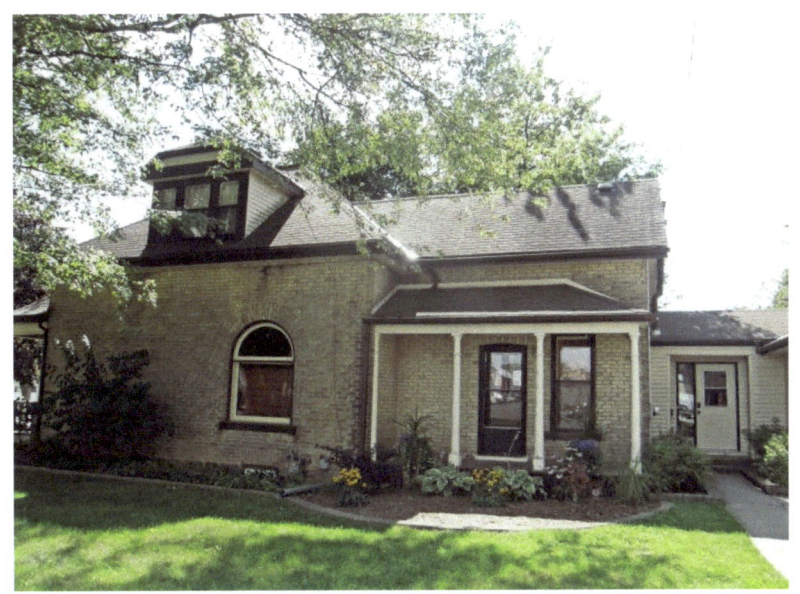
Yellow brick - dormer

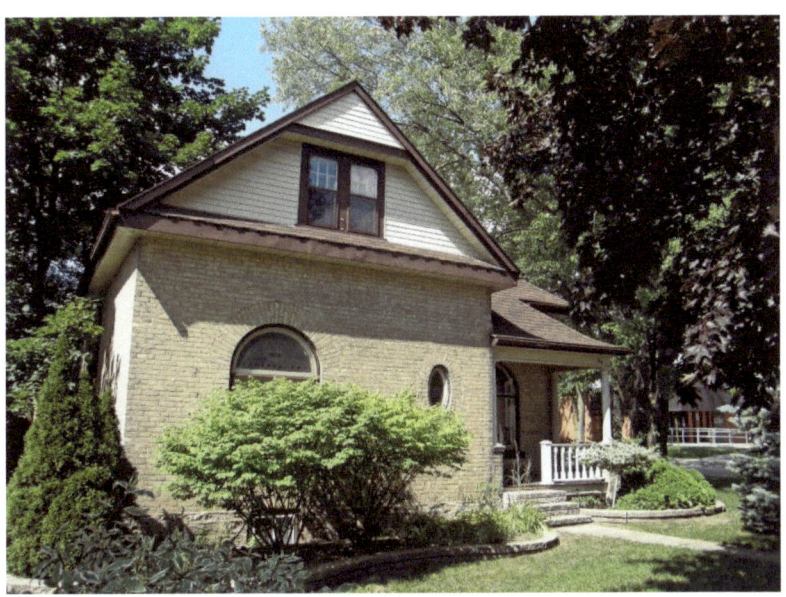
#94 – yellow brick

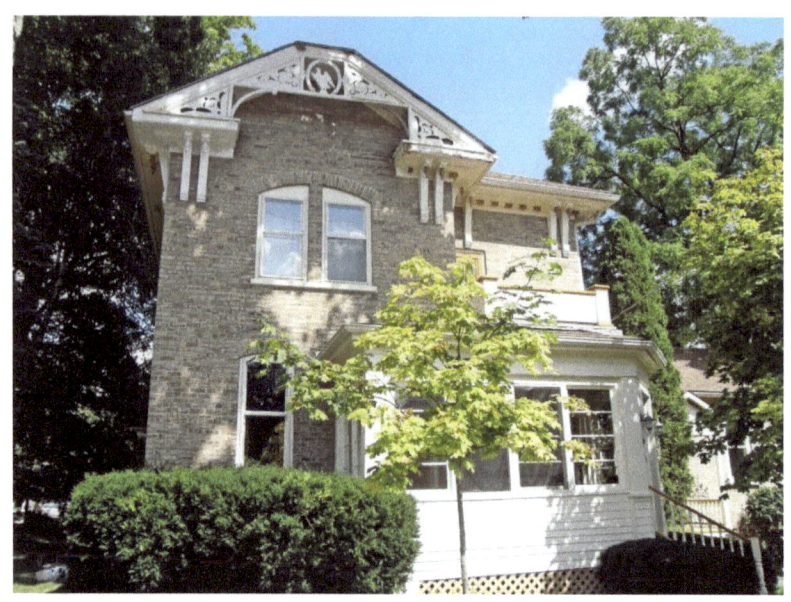

Yellow brick, two storey – verge board, cornice brackets

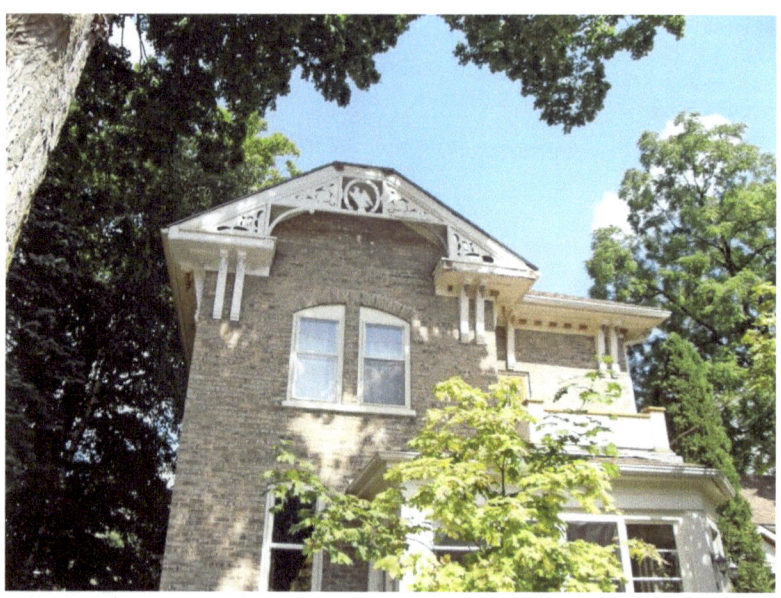

Paired cornice brackets and fancy verge board trim

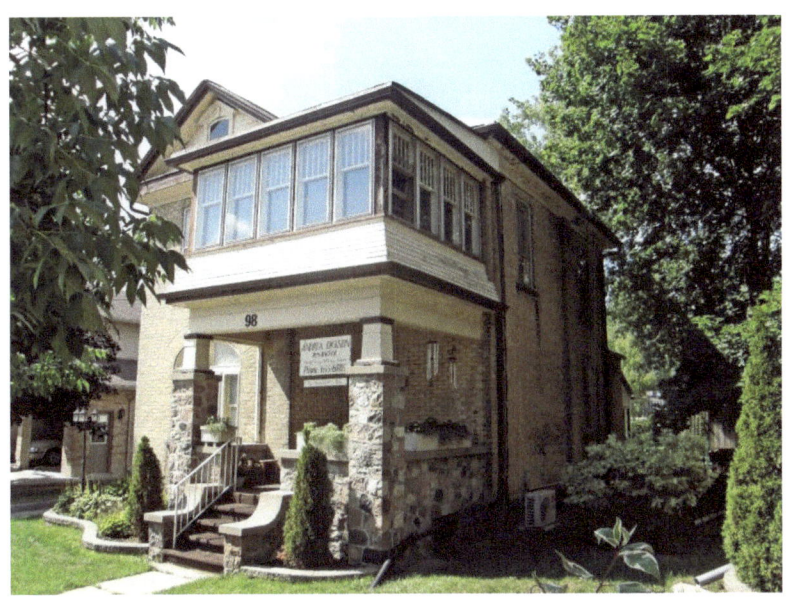

#98 – yellow brick 2½ storey, stone veranda and pillars, enclosed sun porch above veranda

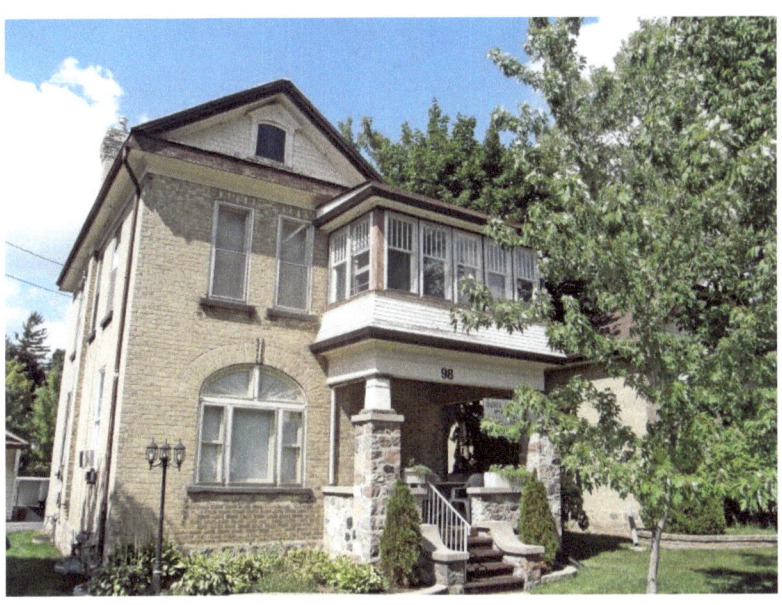

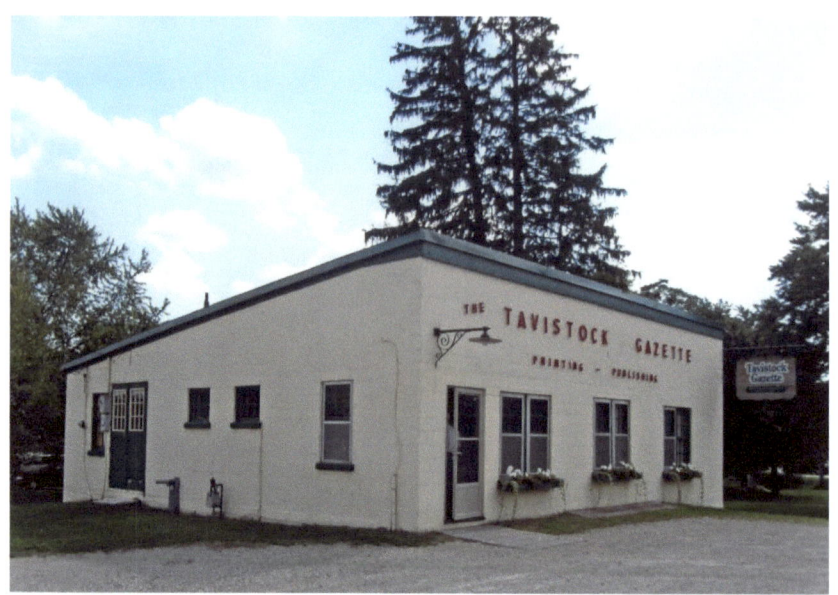

119 Woodstock Street South - Tavistock Gazette

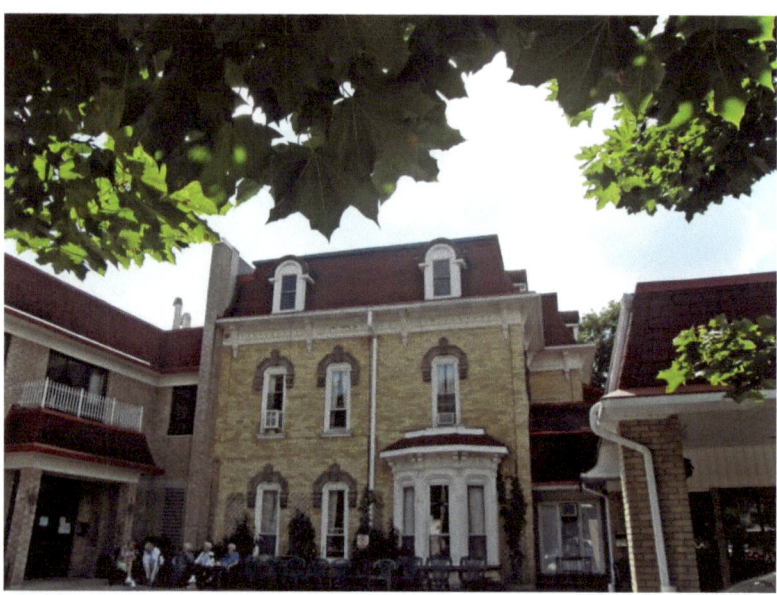

94 William Street - The Maples Home for Seniors – Second Empire – mansard roof, dormers, dripmolds and keystones, bay window

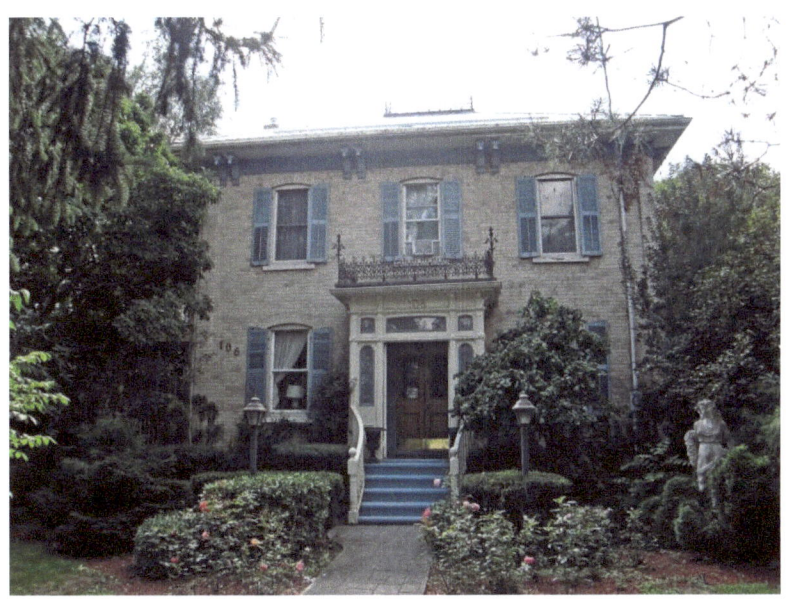

#106 – Neo-Classical style – paired cornice brackets, iron cresting above entrance, shutters

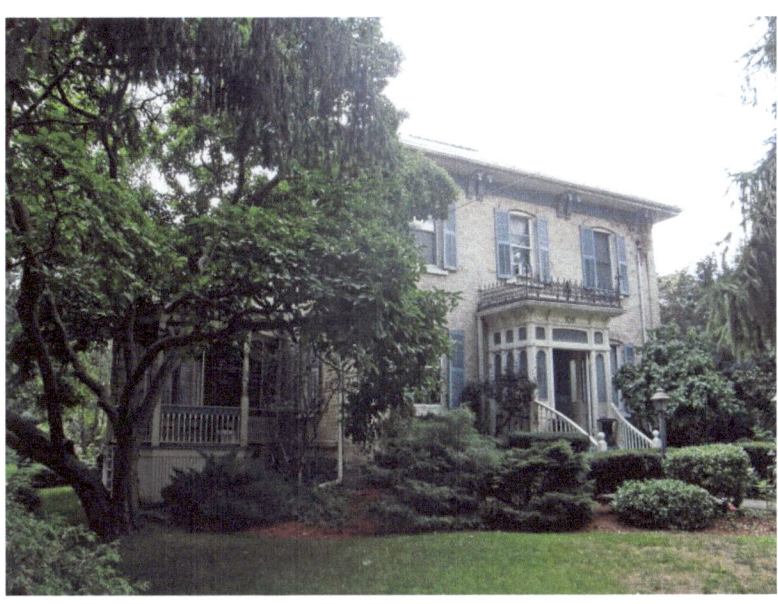

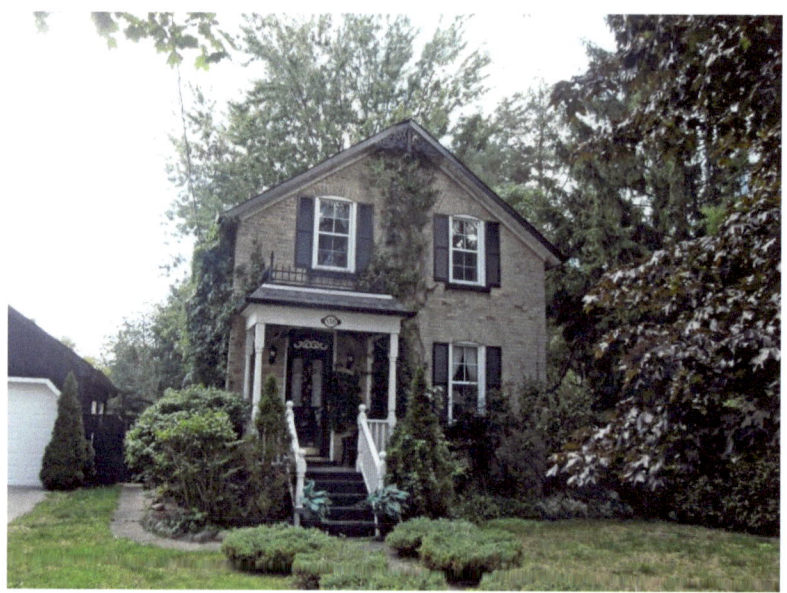

#116 – Gothic - yellow brick, gingerbread trim

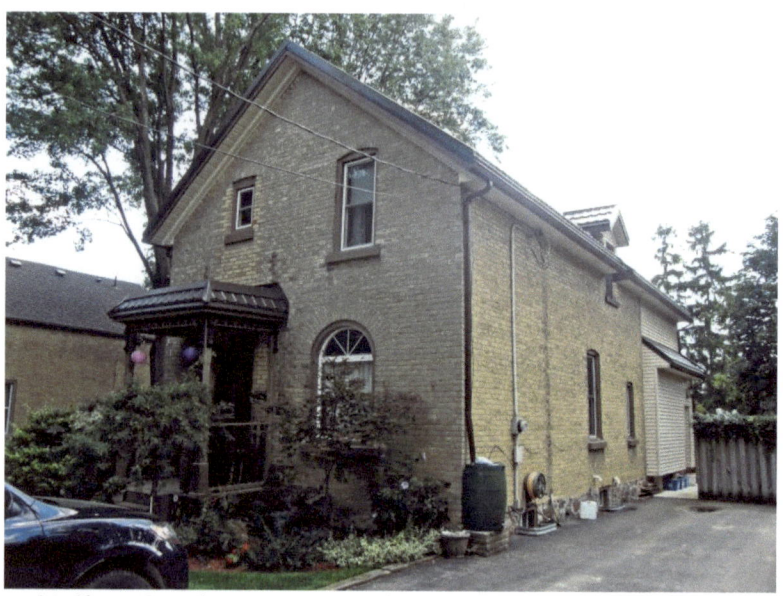

Yellow brick, two storey, dormer window on side

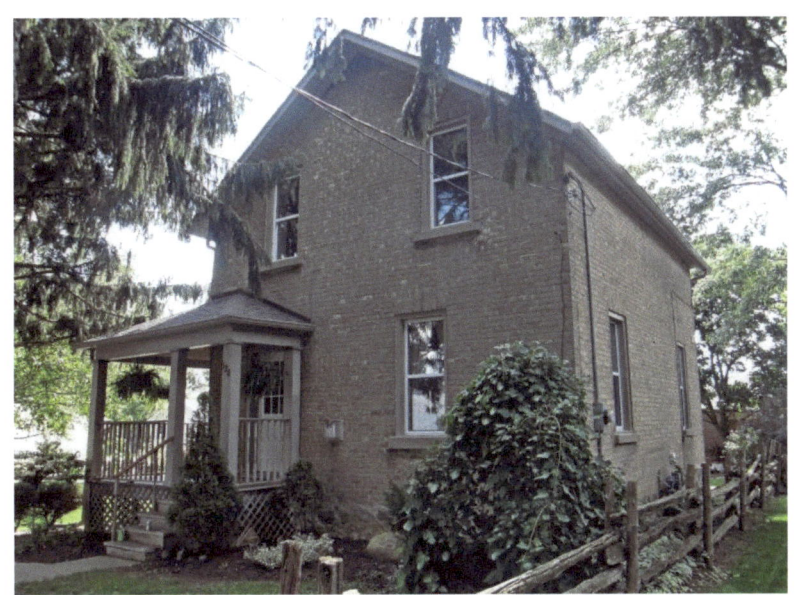

#128 – yellow brick

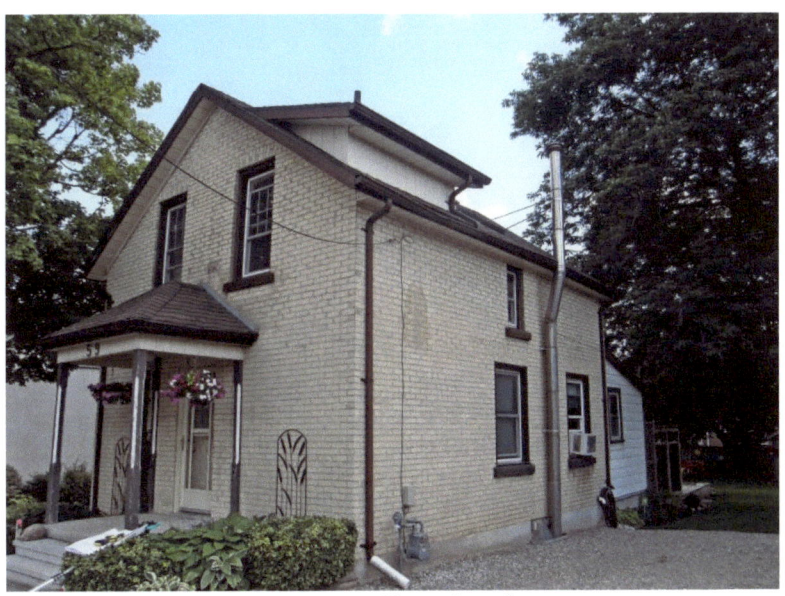

#59 – yellow brick

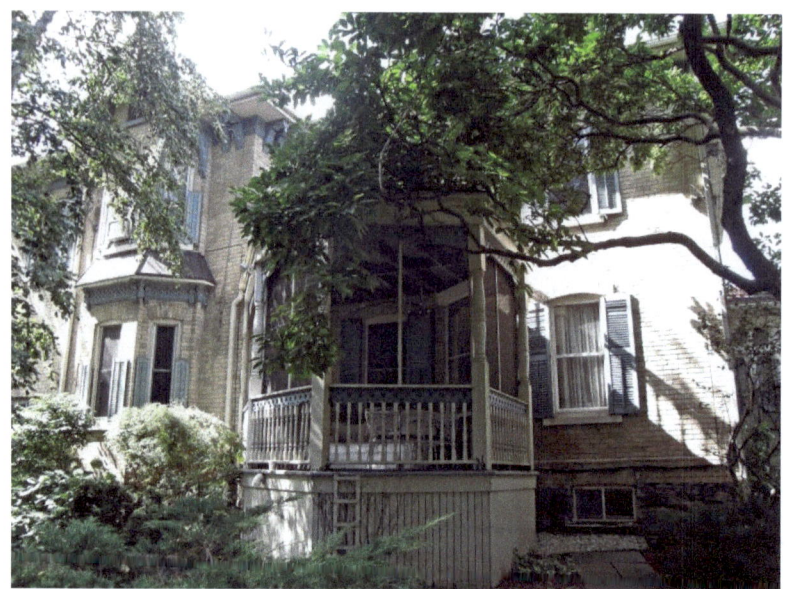

Bay window, shutters

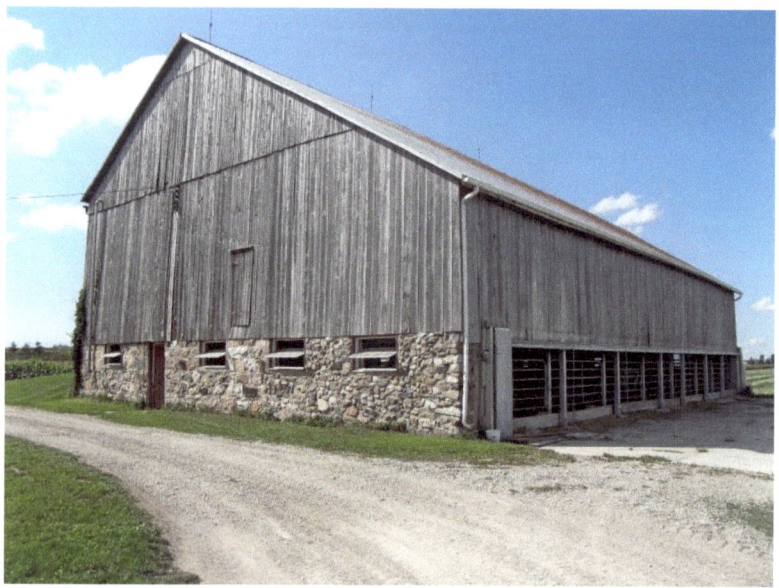

Stone foundation

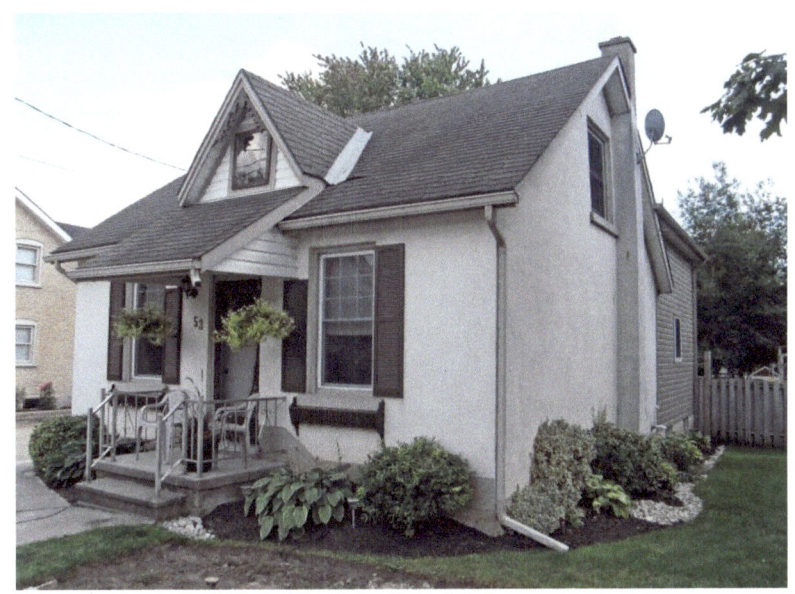
#53 – Gothic Revival cottage

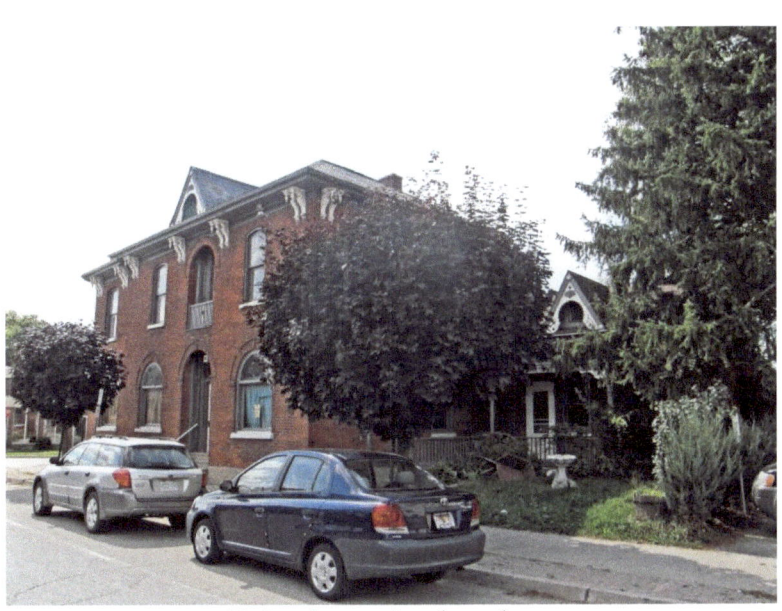
Paired cornice brackets

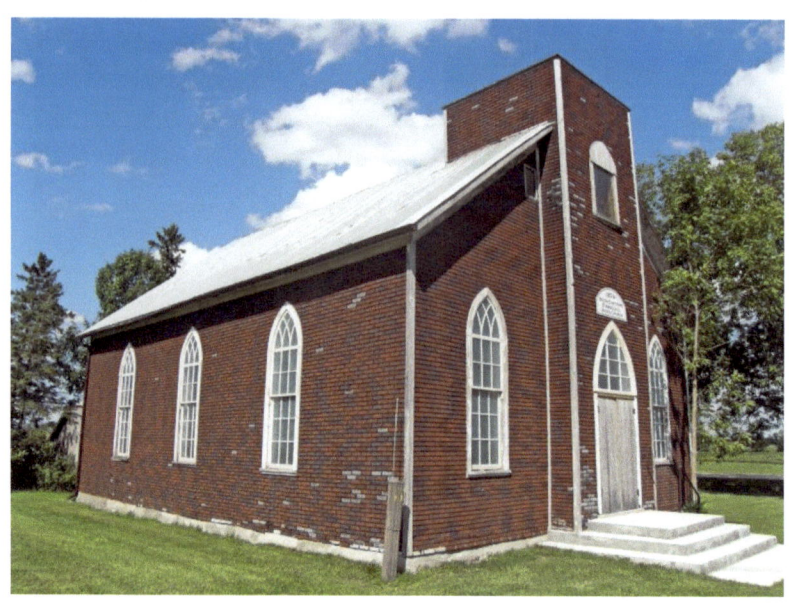

South East Hope Evangelical United – 1874 – Gothic – lancet windows

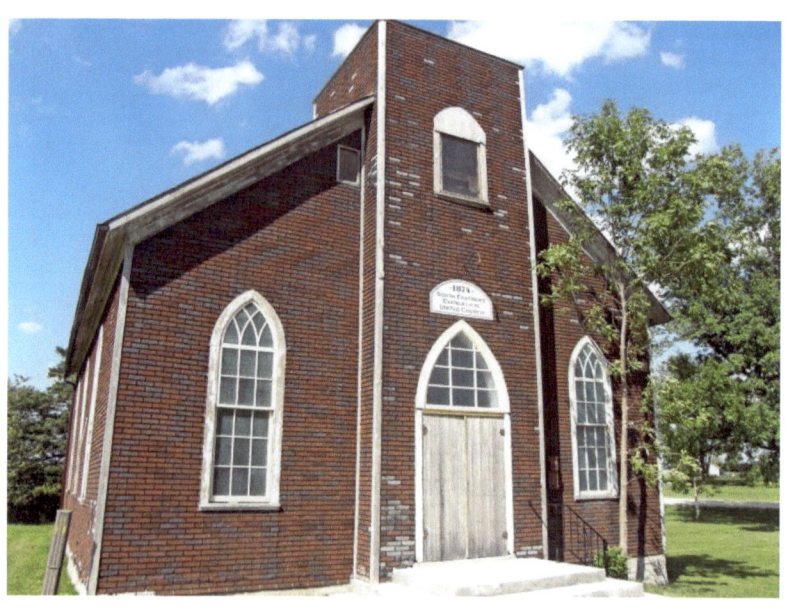

Innerkip

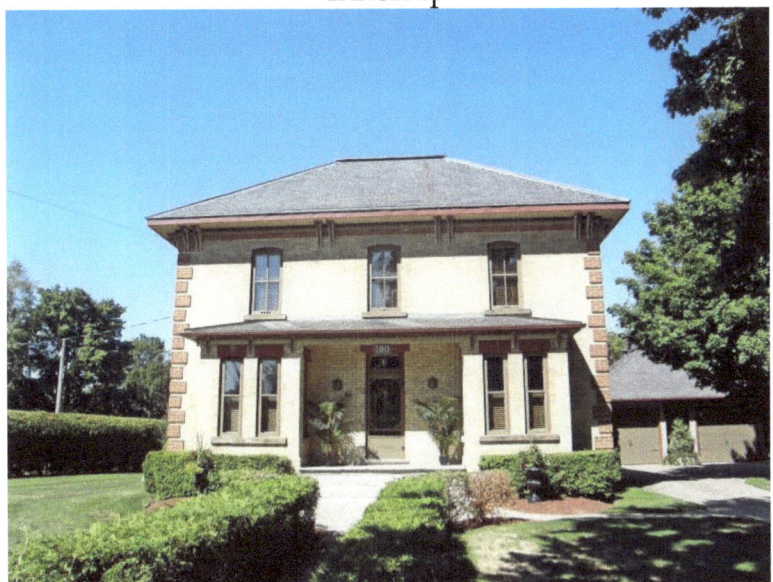

190 Blandford Street – hipped roof, cornice brackets, quoins

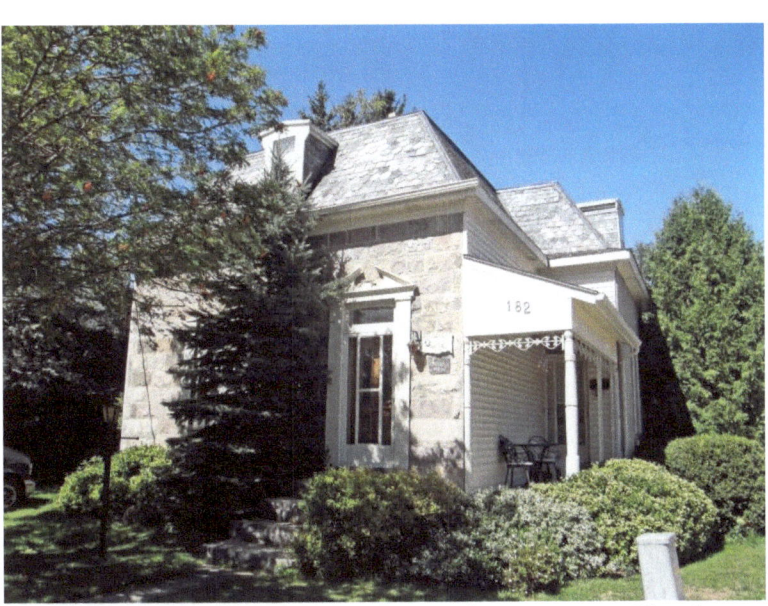

182 Blandford Street – built in 1867 - first owner Charles Vincent – two storey frame house with a stone front and a decorative roof with dormers

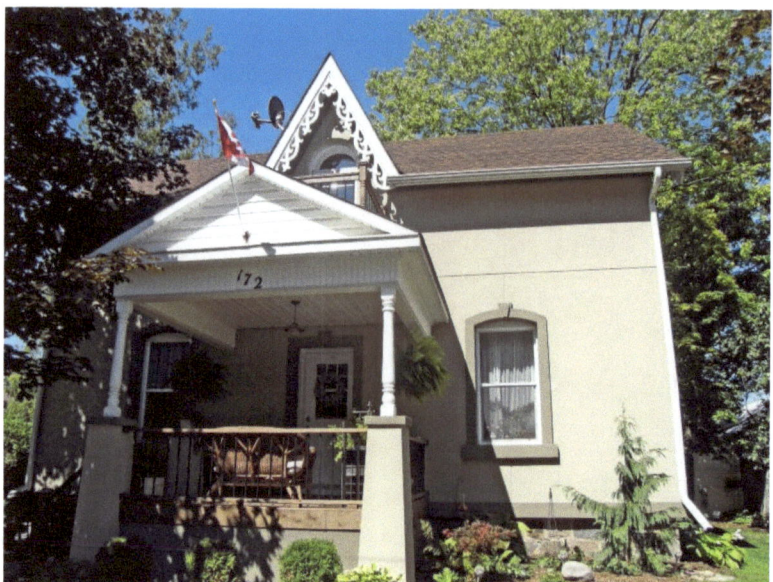

172 Blandford Street – built 1855 - 2 storey home with stone foundation, gingerbread trim on the centre gable, a porch on each floor. The owners welcomed us, showed their home and shared a picnic lunch with us in their backyard.

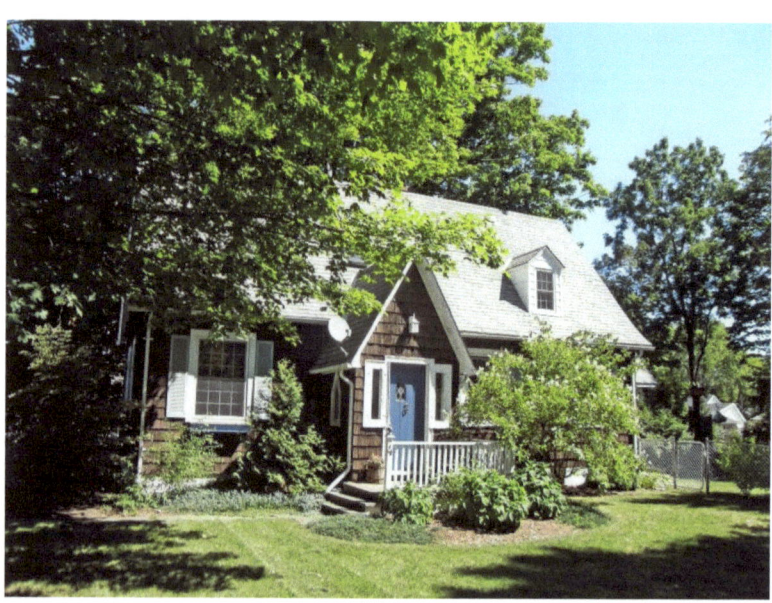

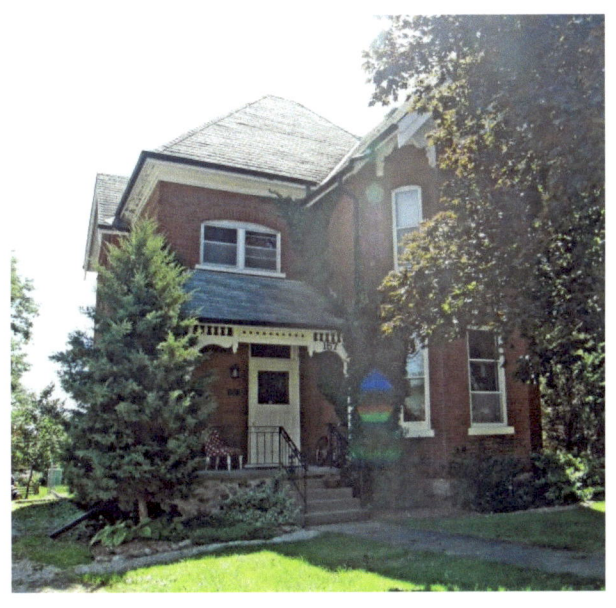

157 Blandford Street – dentil molding, fretwork, 2½-storey tower-like bay

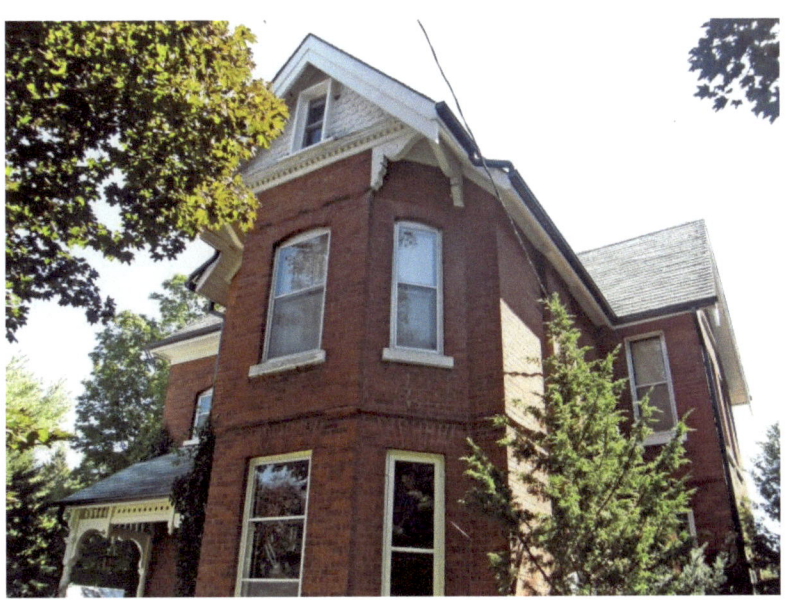

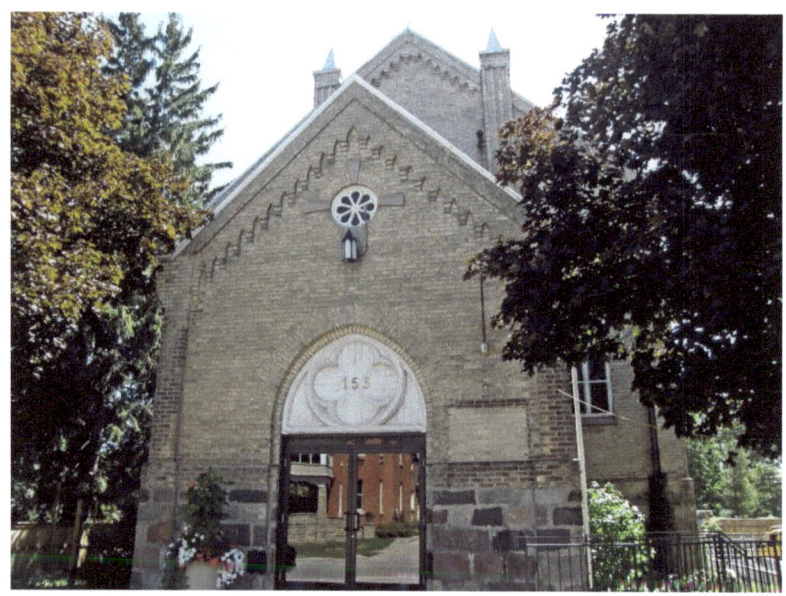

153 Blandford Street – old church – dentil molding, stone foundation

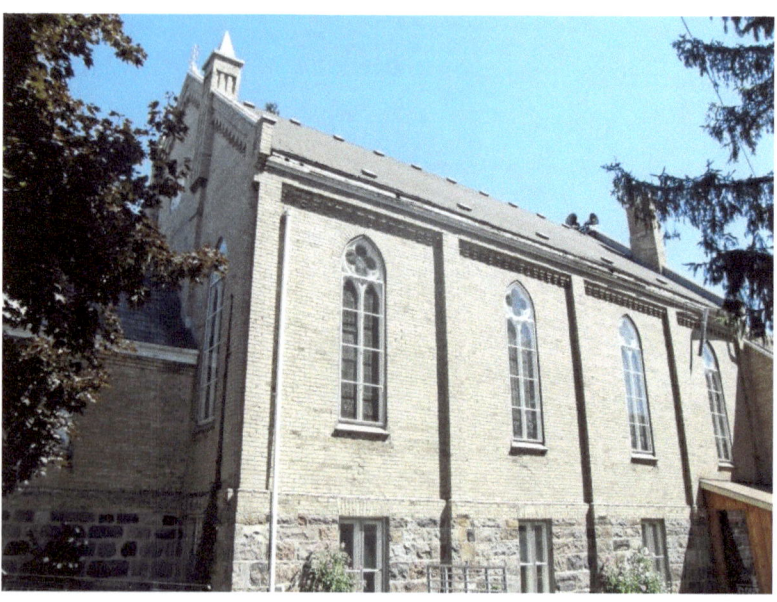

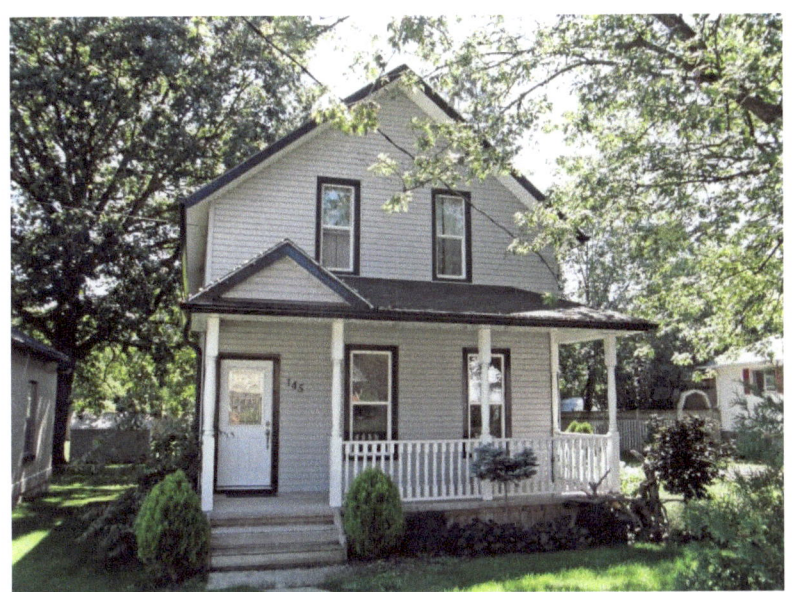
145 Blandford Street

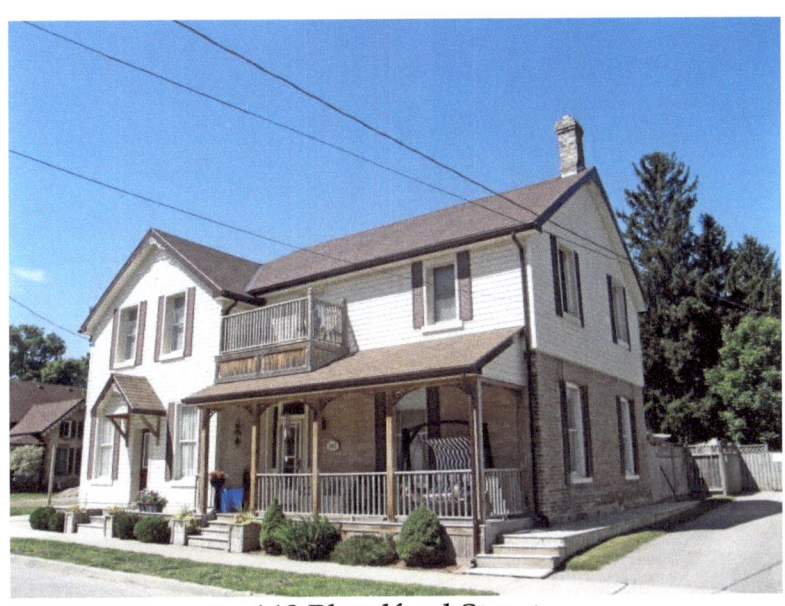
140 Blandford Street

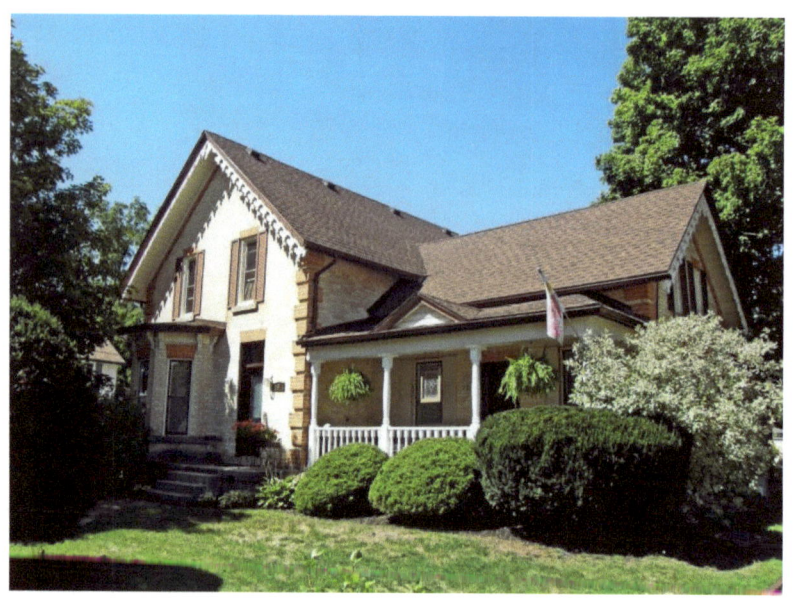

134 Blandford Street – built 1880 - 2 storey yellow brick with red brick corners quoins and red brick above windows, gingerbread trim on gable

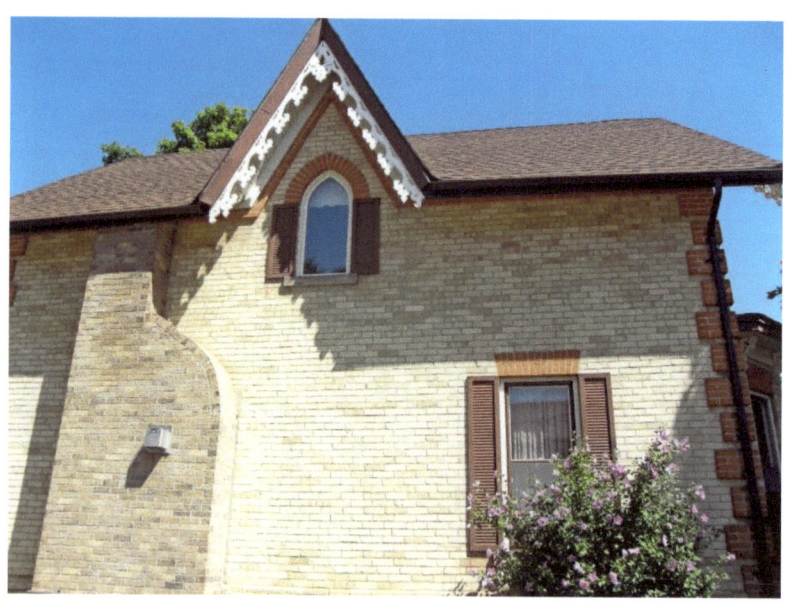

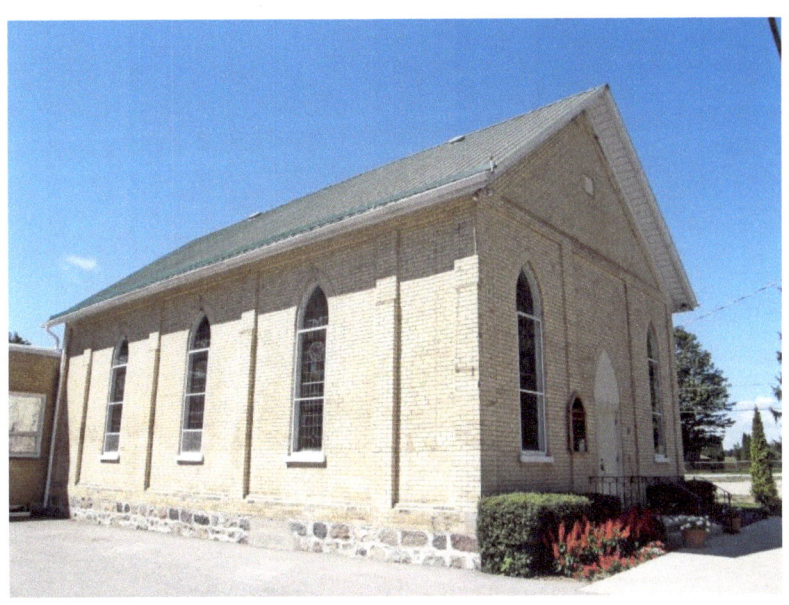

11 Vincent Street - Methodist Church 1886 - Now Innerkip United Church – Gothic – lancet windows, pilasters, stone basement

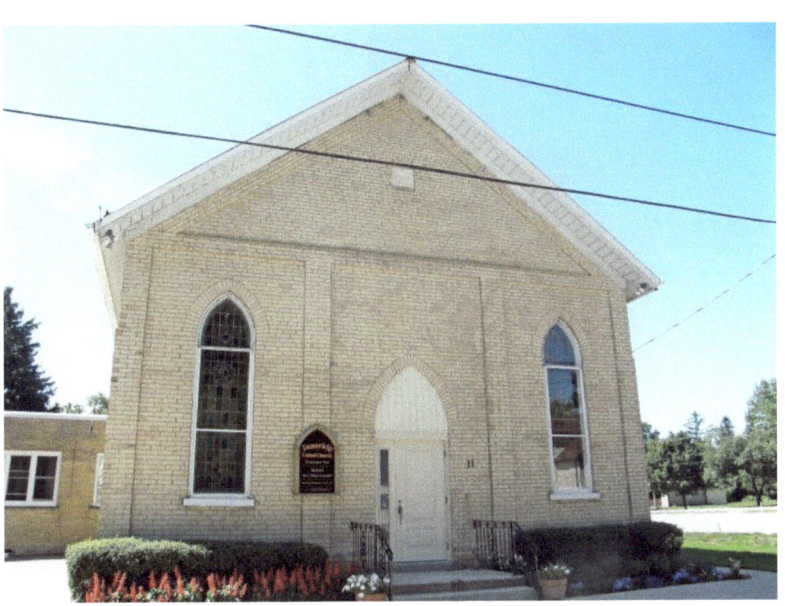

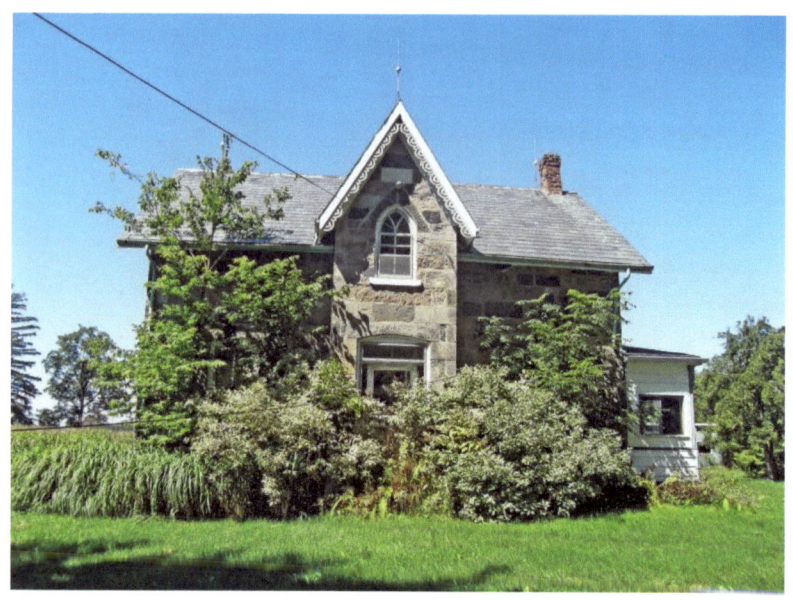

132 Coleman Street – Gothic - built 1888 - 2 storey stone building, steel roof

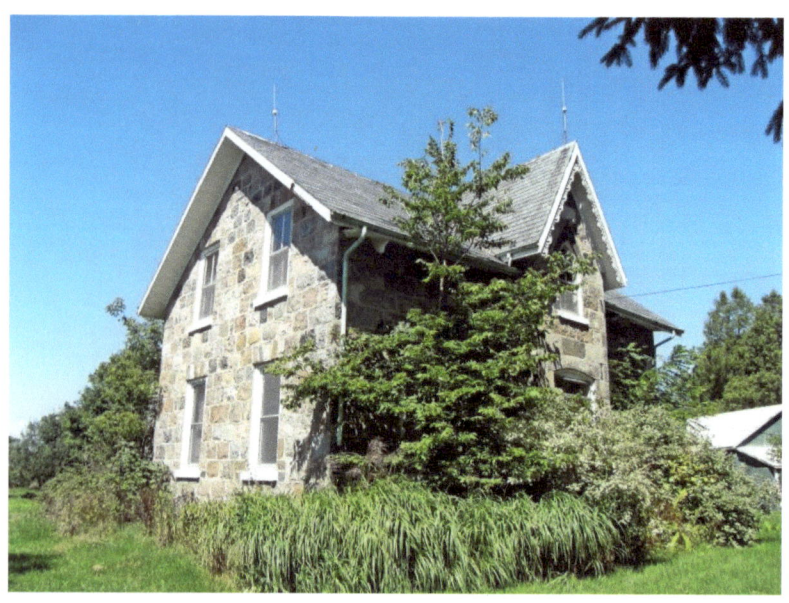

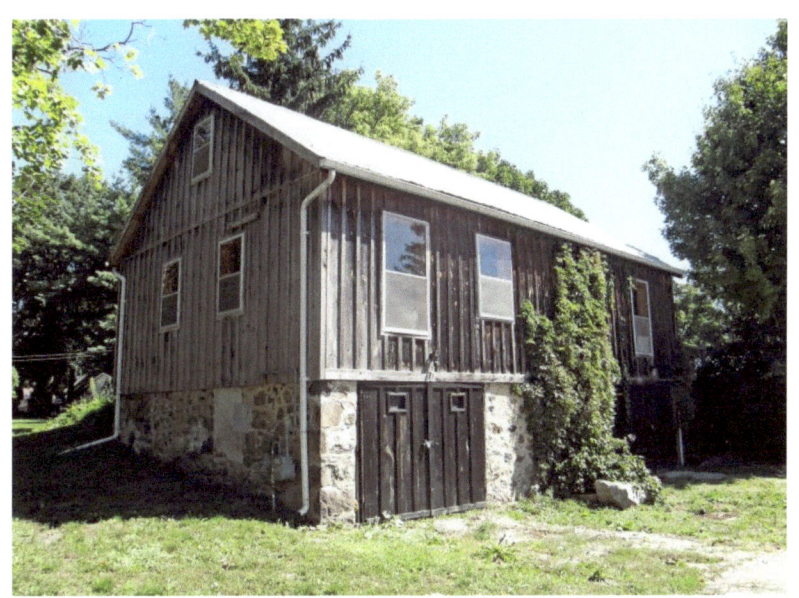

Barn with stone foundation

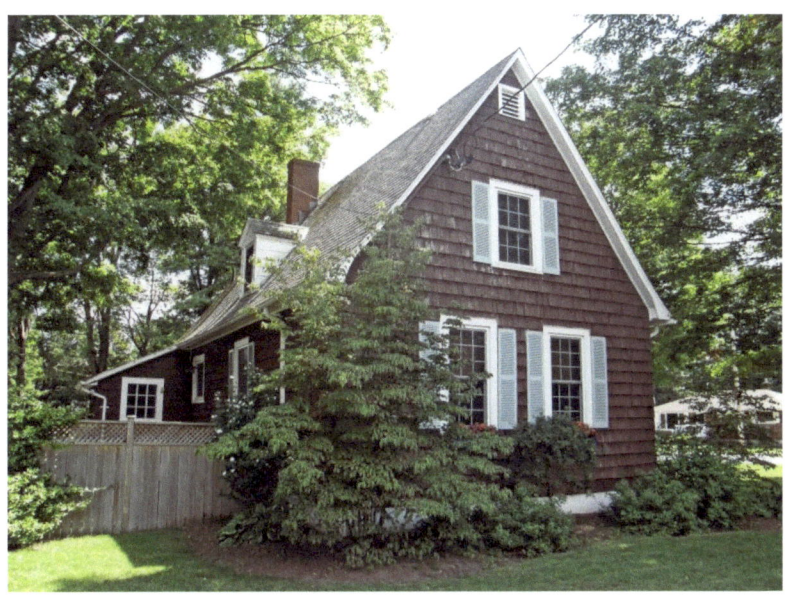

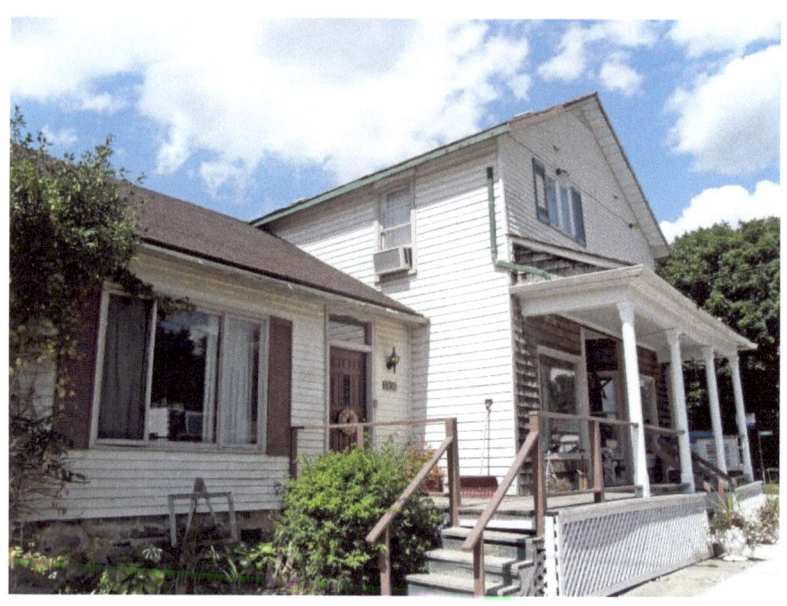

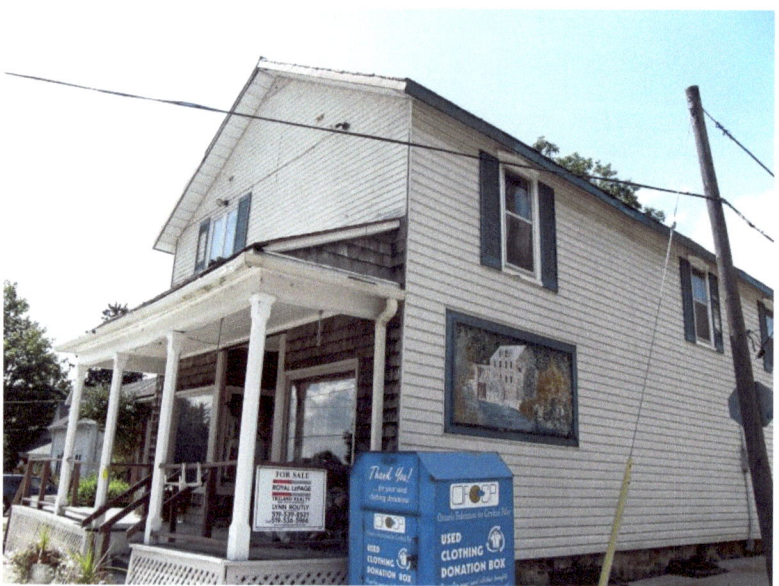

Mural of the old mill on the side of the building

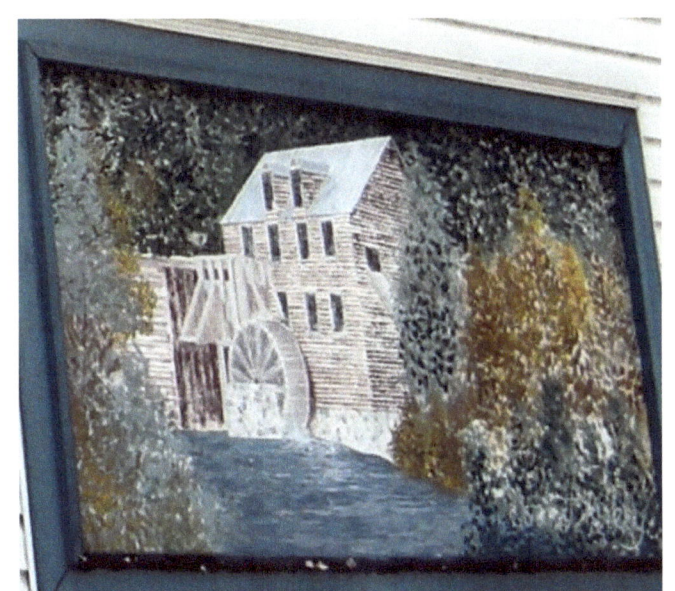
Old mill mural

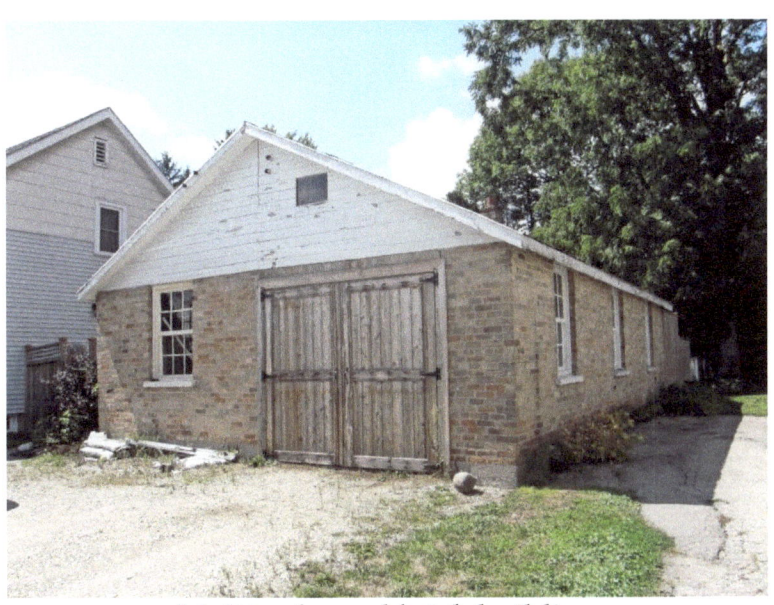
Multi-coloured brick building

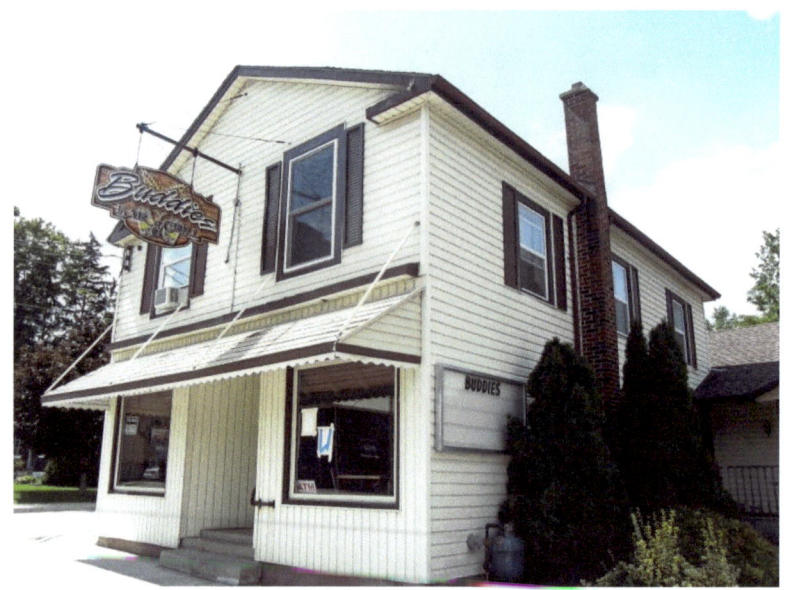

Buddies – cornice return on gable

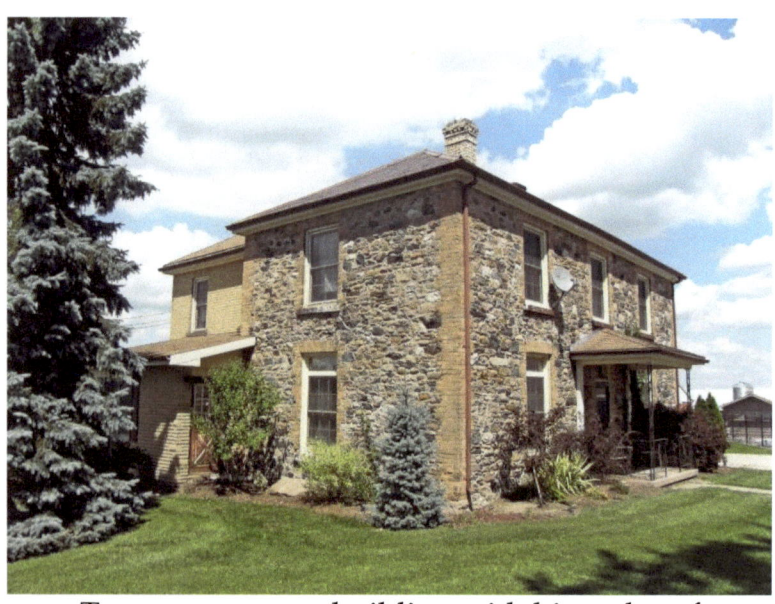

Two-storey stone building with hipped roof

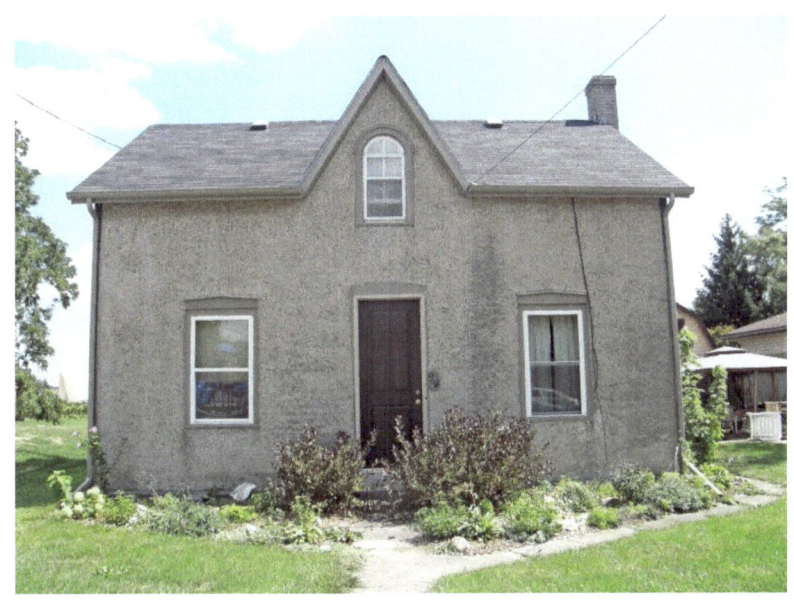

#99 - Gothic Revival style with centre gable

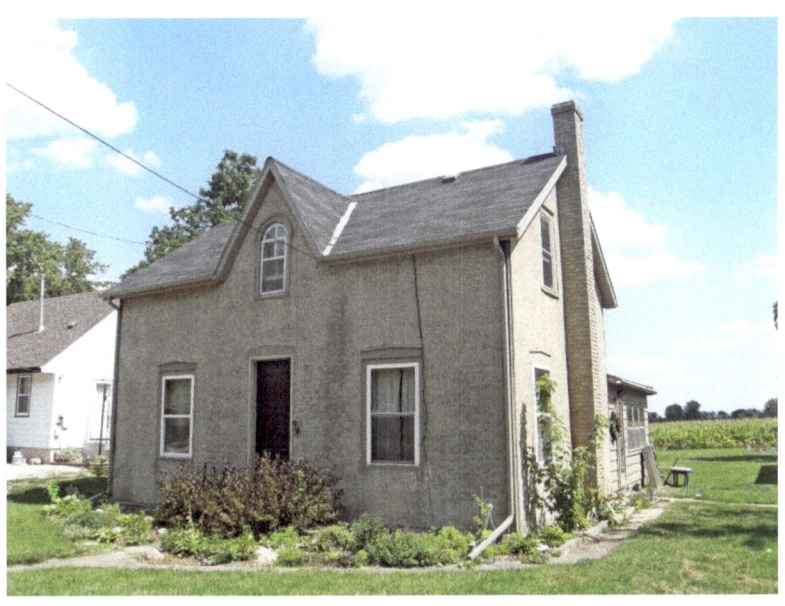

Huntingford

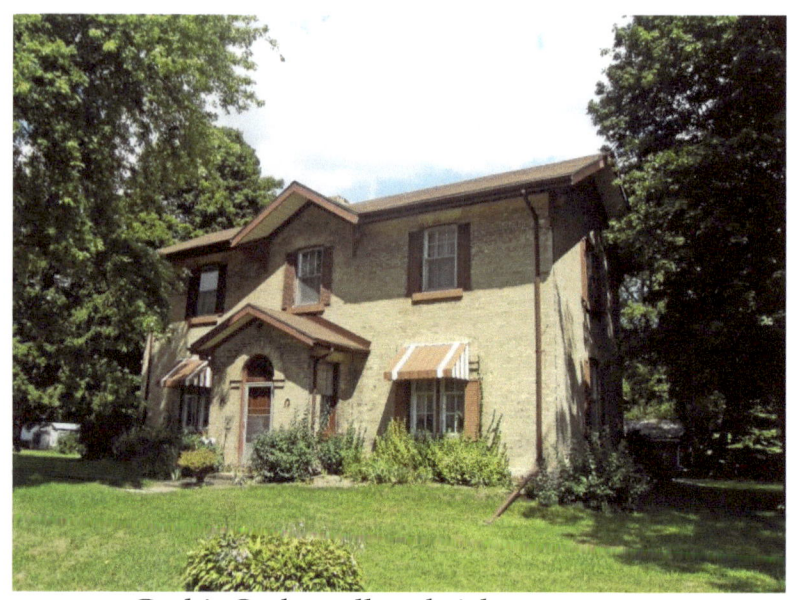

Gothic Style, yellow brick, two storey

Punkydoodles Corners

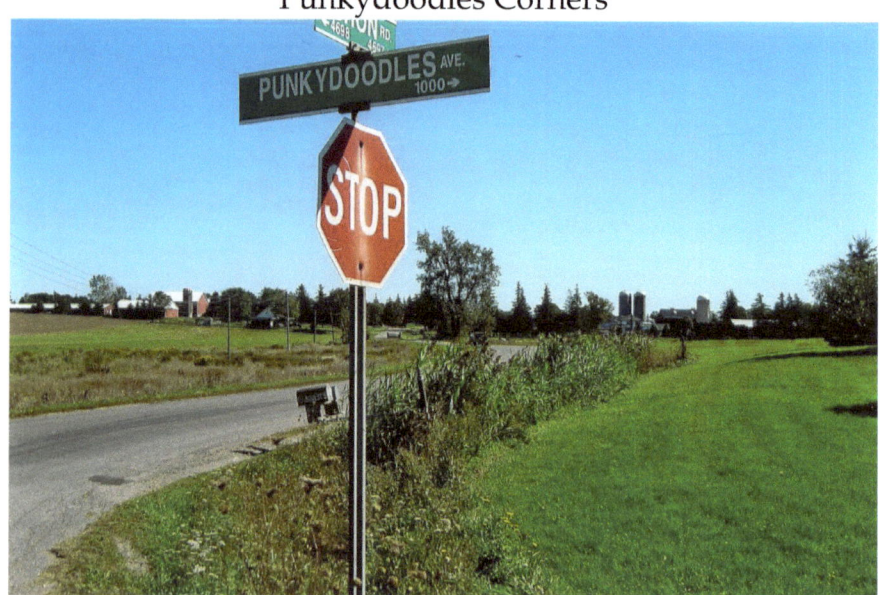

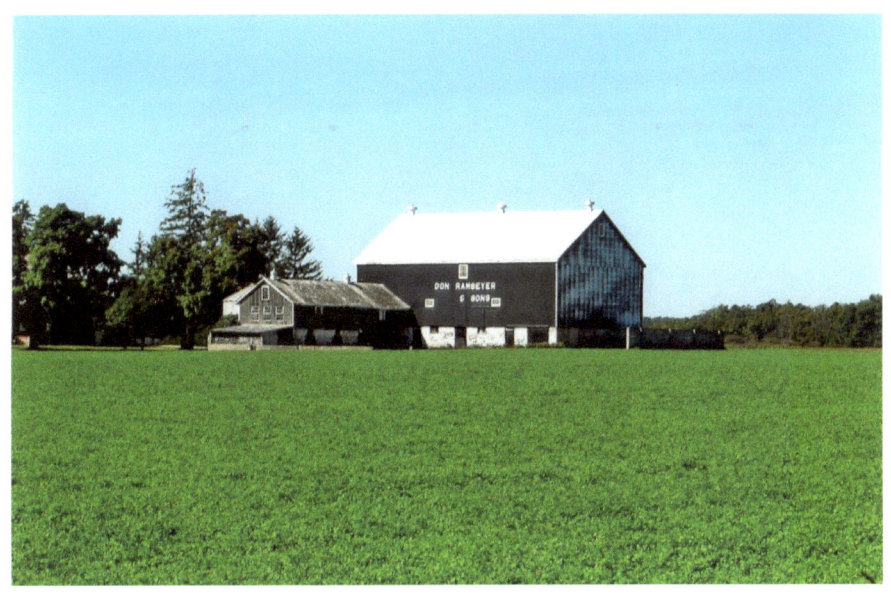

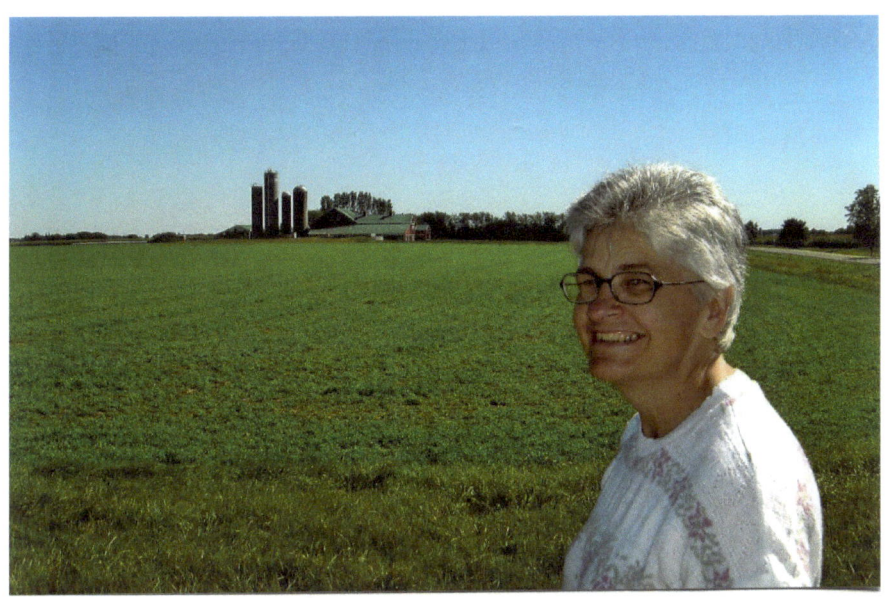

Hickson

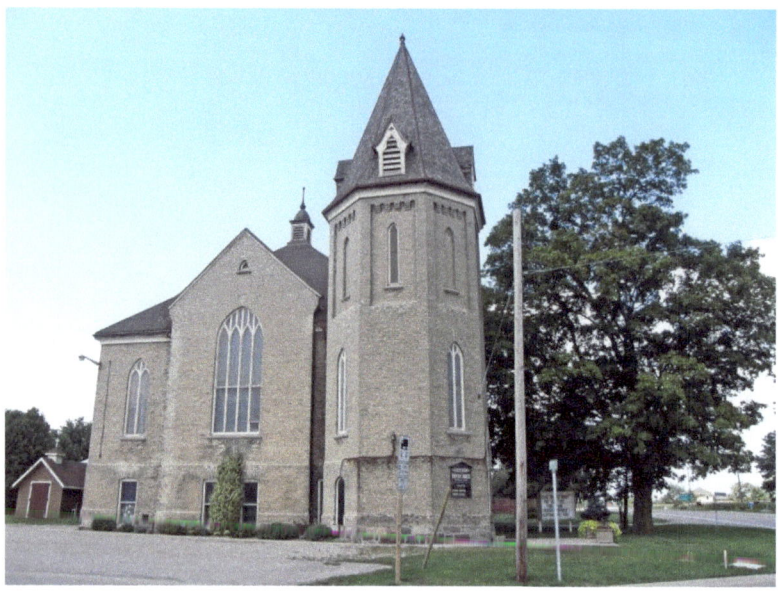

Hickson United Church opened in 1902 as a Wesleyan Methodist Church and joined the United Church in 1925.

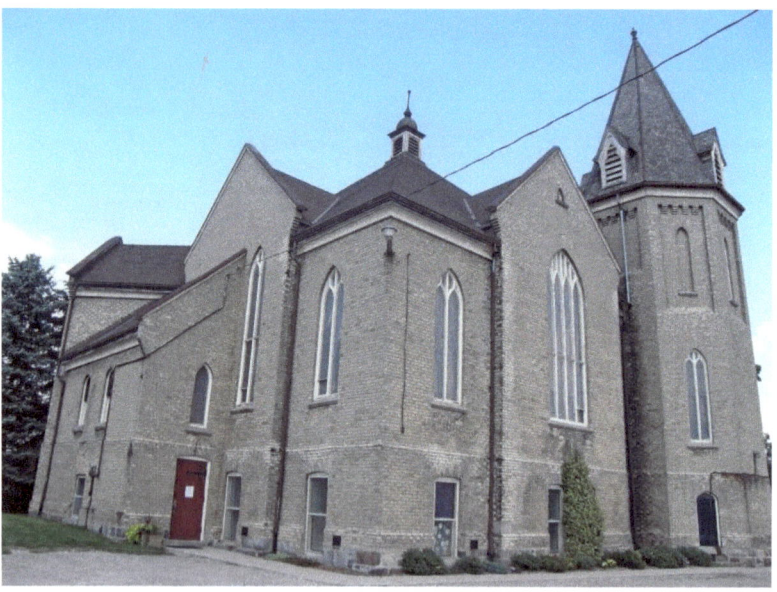

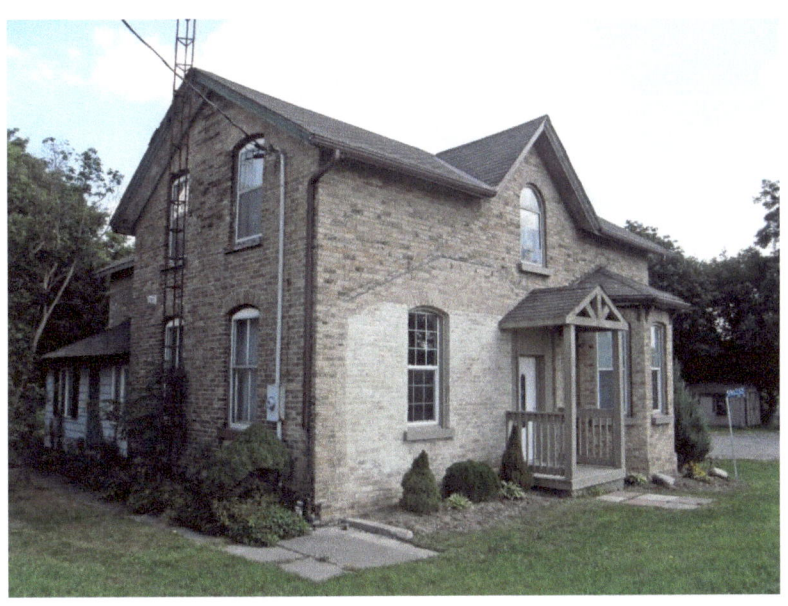

Multi-coloured brick home – Gothic Revival style – bay window with cornice brackets

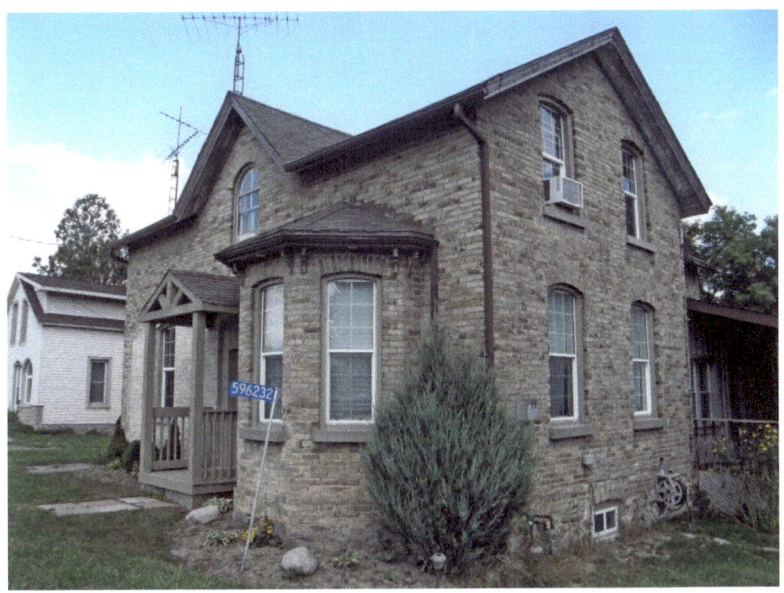

596232

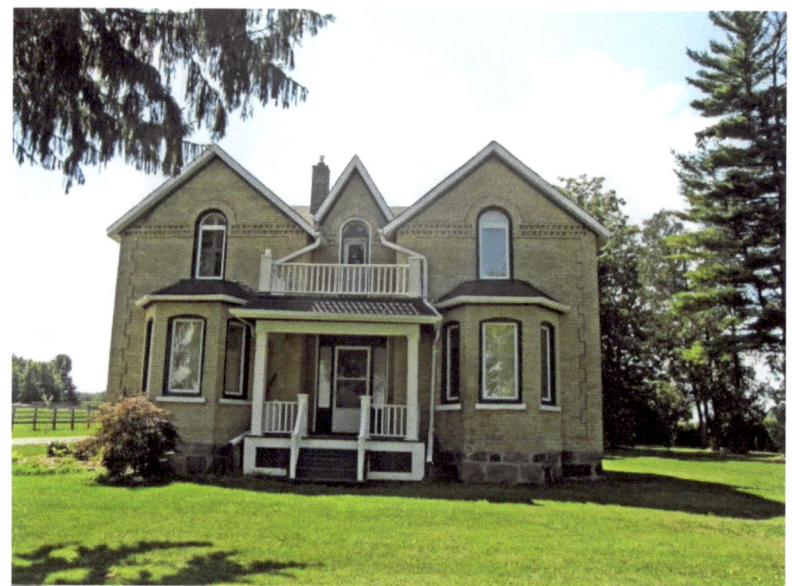

Victorian style, 2 storey, bay windows on lower level, yellow brick, balcony above porch, quoining, voussoirs, decorative brickwork

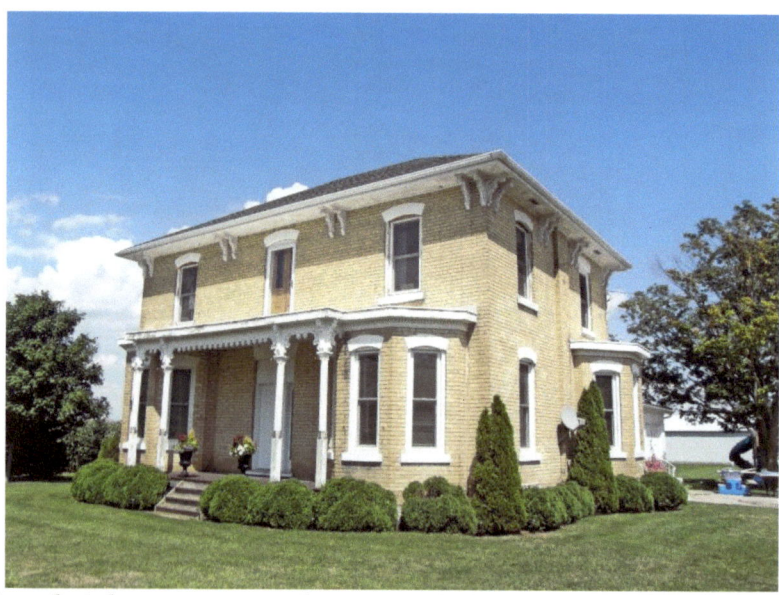

Yellow brick, two-storey home with bay windows on each corner, paired cornice brackets under the eaves, hipped roof

Other Books by Barbara Raue

Coins of Gold
Arrows, Indians and Love
The Life and Times of Barbara
The Cromwell Family Book
Laura Secord Discovered
Daddy Where Are You?

Montana Series
Book 1: Montana Dream
Book 2: Life on the Montana Frontier
Book 3: Montana to Boston and Back
Book 4: Montana Sons Go to War
Book 5: Montana Sons Return from War

Book 1: Rite of Passage
Book 2: Rite of Marriage

© 2019 by Barbara Raue - All the photos in this book have been taken with my cameras. I own the rights to them.

Visit Barbara's website to view all of her books
http://barbararaue.ca

www.ingramcontent.com/pod-product-compliance
Lightning Source LLC
Chambersburg PA
CBHW040244220526
45473CB00001B/359